Outplac

About the author

Max Eggert first read theology at King's College, London before transferring his allegiance to psychology at Birkbeck College and then on to industrial relations at the Polytechnic of Central London. He is a Chartered Psychologist and a Fellow of the Institute of Personnel Management.

With his wife Sian he is Managing Partner of Eggert and Eggert, an international consultancy dedicated to human resources management and outplacement issues based at Lindfield, West Sussex. As an adviser and strategist in the UK and abroad, Max works to enhance the careers of individuals at all levels and backgrounds from both private and public sectors.

The author is married with two children, lives in Sussex and London, and his current passion is riding his grey cob.

For Sian Evans
the best outplacement counsellor and trainer
with whom I have ever been privileged to work

Outplacement

A guide to management and delivery

Max Eggert

May you never need the contents.

Best wishes

Max

March '93.

Institute of Personnel Management

Phototypeset by The Comp-Room, Aylesbury
and printed in Great Britain by
Short Run Press Ltd, Exeter, Devon

British Library Cataloguing in Publication Data

Eggert, Max
Outplacement : a guide to management and delivery.
I. Title
650.14

ISBN 0 85292 468 2

The views expressed in this book are the author's own, and may not necessarily reflect those of the IPM.

Contents

Foreword

I found this book a compulsive read. In dealing with outplacement and all its related external activities, Max Eggert skilfully avoids unnecessary jargon and puts across his message in plain English.

Outplacement should not be used merely as a salvage operation for career shipwrecks during recession. Strategically employed before, during and after re-organization, it can provide management with a valuable tool to aid job mobility and to help employees cope with it. Since the job-for-life concept is now moribund, career counselling and outplacement will always be needed.

Max offers straightforward, easily understood advice throughout. Redundancies, he suggests, for example, should always be announced 'on Tuesday or Wednesday'. It is the immediate superior who, given proper training, should normally be responsible for releasing an individual. Neither does he mince words. There is always a danger, he warns, that redundancy can provide 'an open season for managerial expression of subjective criteria for selection or settling of old scores'. He deals fairly and non-judgementally with some of the controversial 'political' issues such as the 'corporate' versus 'retail' argument which centres on the view of one sector that it is unethical to take fees directly from (and hence give professional guidance to) redundant individuals who have not been paid for by their previous employer.

In offering this comprehensive overview of outplacement, Max Eggert has, for the first time, combined a broad managerial perspective on organizational change with an insider's grasp of the specialist skills.

I welcome this book.

Terry Lyons
Chairman of the IPM National Forum for Counselling and Outplacement

Preface

This book is written for human resource managers and senior line executives who are involved in the difficult issues of releasing individuals from their organizations and who wish to provide those who lose their job with appropriate help. 'Outplacement' is the term used to describe the assistance given to individuals who lose their job. The significant issues of outplacement are examined in four basic sections, beginning with an introduction which looks at what outplacement is and is not. The management of outplacement is the subject of the next section, which is for those wanting to get the best from outplacement as purchasers of the service. Individual concerns around job loss make up the third section, and the delivery of outplacement forms the final section. The book ends on some post-outplacement issues and a glossary.

Outplacement is essentially a 'soft' subject, which is to say that no two situations are ever the same. Rather like a jellyfish: difficult to describe, even more difficult to get hold of, but one would be unwise to ignore it. In outplacement there are no absolute rules of procedure, only principles and ways of approaching individuals and situations which seem to work because they have been born of experience rather than theory or research.

Whilst the structure of the book follows an idealized operational chronology, outplacement situations are born of crisis and significant change, so projects develop sequences of their own which frequently defy logic or reason. Once started, it is as if the Human Resources department is constantly running to catch up, and when it reaches the goalposts they move. Prescription is not appropriate to this topic, so what follows is mainly advice and insights gained from the scar tissue of real situations. Even when there is theory it is kept to a minimum, but for those who wish to take the subject further a basic bibliography is provided. Essentially outplacement is about people, not theory, and if I have got it right now it is because I got it wrong before. Consultants always learn at their clients' expense.

This book is dedicated to the task of sharing with those who have responsibility for people in organizations how to go about what must be the most difficult and certainly the most distasteful of all management responsibilities; that is, making jobs redundant and putting those who do them out into the cold. It is my hope that the book will go some way to make redundancy, for those who have to implement it, less onerous and consequently, for those who have to suffer it, less painful.

M.A.E.
November 1991

Acknowledgements

No one can write even a small book like this on their own. The thousands of people that I have worked with over the past decade and who have given me the privilege of working with them in the important aspects of their careers have all contributed. I came to outplacement through John Talbot and Anne McQuade of EMAS, so I am grateful to them. Also my association with Pauline Hyde as director of group work and a brief spell working with Chris Dunn at TDA helped inordinately. To these my mentors and colleagues my thanks. Special gratitude to Tony Milne of CEPEC, and John Hall of Peat Marwick, John Flouch of CEPEC and Neil Killion of PHA Australia, all of whom contributed to my commitment and growth more than they will ever know. In this line of work you learn from your team and colleagues as much as they learn from you and whilst there is insufficient space to mention all, my thanks go to Jane Slemeck, Dave Parish, Sid Hilsum, Bill Huddleston, Geoff Brown, Jenny Heather, Christine Standring, Fokkina MacDonnell, Penny Swinburne, Susan Williams, Madeline McGill, Gillian England, Brian Errington, Terry Lyons, Jon Lawton, Val Lowman, Chris Cocks, Jo Ousten and Beverley Kissoon, all of whom have contributed to my knowledge and skills in the subject area. Consultants also learn from clients, so here I must mention Bob White, Judy Mills, Ros Blackburn, Ian Butler, Bob Ward and Robin Wayman, again for their contribution to my growth. Finally, to Kathy Parkes and Humphrey Evans for their background support.

I feel totally gutted and so ashamed. They had the best years of my life and now they throw me out.

Manufacturing supervisor

Who is going to want me now I have no postdoctoral research experience and at 29 I am burnt out?

PhD, computer specialist

I got to where I was by hard work, not qualifications. I will never get a similar job with only three GCSEs.

Money trader

It just seemed to be the best thing to do. I could not tell anybody, so for eight hours a day I went to the service station at South Mimms. I couldn't face telling my family and friends I was out of a job.

Accounting supervisor

They must have known I was leaving a good job to join them, so why did they take me on six months ago only to make me redundant now?

Salesman, electronics

How could they do this to me? Why? Our families have known each other for the past twenty years.

Foreman, playing-card manufacturer

Forgive me for putting you through this, but I did not have the strength to endure the pain that was coming.

Chris Donahue's suicide note, written after receiving notice of redundancy

Chapter 1
Introduction

Why outplacement is important

It may be apocryphal but in the early 1960s it was claimed that the management of General Motors stated to its employees, 'Be loyal to the Company and the Company will be loyal to you.' Employees as individuals can only work from the experience they have, and those who joined their employer in the 1950s, '60s and '70s got used to and anticipated continuous employment. In those days a job was for ever. People who were made redundant were looked at very carefully, as if their condition was a direct outcome of their performance or lack of it at work.

During the '80s things changed radically. The manufacturing base in the UK was significantly reduced, with many hourly paid and skilled employees and those who managed them being released from their firms as they closed down. Now in the '90s it is the service sector and higher management levels that are being shaken out as both private and public sectors attempt to be lean and mean and embrace the contingencies of a rigorous market economy. The music of mergers is not the song of the work force but tunes of business performance criteria, of economies of scale and shareholder ratios.

The numbers and impact are considerable. Eighteen hundred people in the small community of Uddingston, east of Glasgow, lost their jobs when Caterpillar, a US multinational producing large earth-moving equipment, decided to close its Scottish operation. Thousands are leaving British Telecom, and all the major banks in Britain have programmes to lose tens of thousands. Hospitals under the trust arrangements are letting hundreds of people go. Recent estimates in America record that 10 per cent of the total work force are affected each year by downsizing, merger or acquisition-related activity. Britain is quickly catching up. Each day announcements of job losses are made.

Even when mergers or buy-outs are not successful the effects in terms of jobs and people can be legion. When it beat off a take-over by Sir James Goldsmith, the Anglo-French financier, in the late '80s, Goodyear, the largest tyre manufacturer in the world, released about 4,300 employees worldwide and about the same amount through natural wastage and freezes on recruitment. The halcyon days of labour pooling are gone for ever, it would seem. In these matters the numbers come first and the human factors last. Changes are financially driven, or market-driven, or client-driven, and the costs in human terms come way down in the hierarchy of issues for consideration.

The costs to individuals who are forced to leave (and even those who stay) in downsized and merged organizations are colossal. Individuals lose not only their income but their pride, their self-respect and their confidence (see the sections on the psychology and stages of job loss). Their families also suffer. Those who remain are also affected in ways that can be both debilitating and devastating. They feel betrayed by their managers, they lose their loyalty and the more able but disaffected display their dissatisfaction by leaving (this is covered in the section on the survivor syndrome, page 132).

It is said that for as long as seven years after the merger between Rank and Xerox executives were being labelled as either 'Rankers' or 'Xeroids'. As Stuart Lydall, chief executive at the large Welwyn Garden City site of the merged pharmaceutical firm, SmithKline Beecham, commented on the difference between a merger and an acquisition, 'In an acquisition you only upset half the people.' There is now substantial agreement among researchers that success in post-downsizing, merger or acquisition is dependent upon how individuals and groups within the remaining organization work together. Consequently, it is how the organization goes about its closure, merger and acquisition activity that is crucial to its continuing success.

What is it?

Outplacement is not a popular term. Even those who provide outplacement services do not like this American jargon. Unfortunately, in spite of attempts to call the process or service something different, the term remains persistent in the extreme. What is outplacement? A working definition could be something like this:

> *Outplacement.* The process whereby an individual or individuals compelled to leave their employer are given support and counselling to assist them in achieving the next stage of their career.

Outplacement consists essentially in assisting people through the transitional period after job loss, that is, when they have left their current employment until the next stage. For the individual the next stage is usually a similar job to the previous one, but increasingly as jobs disappear it may be a different position or career where existing skills can be utilized or developed. Individuals occasionally choose to do something completely different when their original job has become redundant; some choose active retirement and so may go 'plural', holding several jobs at the same time.

The word 'compelled' in the definition needs some explanation. The usual compulsion comes from redundancy, but there are other forms such as enforced early retirement or being invited to resign. More and more individual, usually senior, employees are outplacing themselves by choosing not to continue working for a particular organization. Frequently, as a major acquisition or merger goes through, individuals ask to be outplaced because they do not wish to be part of the new venture.

Essentially, outplacement is a supportive and empowering process. The responsibility for choosing, pursuing and securing a new future remains the responsibility of the individual, with the outplacement consultancy providing support and guidance through each stage of the process. Those who provide outplacement are thought of as counsellors rather than trainers, advisers rather than teachers, for the essential decisions concerning career direction always remain with the individual and not with those providing the outplacement.

Outplacement services fall neatly into two major market sectors – corporate and retail. Essentially the difference between the two lies in who pays for the services. Corporate outplacement services are paid for by the organization which is releasing the individual – outplacement services then being part of the separation package, along with statutory payments, loyalty bonus and other benefits. Retail outplacement is different because it is funded by the individual, who pays directly for the outplacement service which is received. The service itself is essentially the same: the major difference is one of funding. Some large consultancies work exclusively for the corporate sector and have a code which precludes them from dealing with retail (see page 159). Most consultancies, even the large ones such as Inter Exec, provide services for both corporate and retail. Since HR managers will be looking for support for their employees, the book will mainly focus on issues attendant to the corporate sector. However, where a firm will not or cannot provide employee support the HR manager will wish to refer those being released to appropriate retail programmes so a watchful eye on what is being offered and quality issues is valid for this market as well.

Lewis Rushbrook, a consultant with the large outplacement firm CEPEC, has pointed out that responsibilities are also different within the employing organization. A company wanting to release senior executives will approach an outplacement organization, while a company *seeking* senior executives will retain a recruitment organization. It follows that the direction of professional accountability also differs. Outplacement consultancies are professionally responsible to the previous employer, while recruitment organizations are beholden to a candidate's future employer. Preserving this distinction between outplacement and recruitment organizations is fundamental if conflicts of interest are to be avoided. In fact the real loyalty of the counsellor is to the individual who is being outplaced and needs help, not exclusively to the previous employer who, as the client, is picking up the tab.

Getting a job is a painful process. Job hunting is a solitary activity, and being continually turned down is not the best thing to happen to someone who has just been put out of work. Outplacement is valuable not just in the mechanics of getting a job but in handling the dark nights of unemployment, of feeling useless, unwanted and of no worth. Pauline Hyde, one of the founders of outplacement in the UK, was fond of saying that her job was putting the stuffing back into people. Tom Carew, the doyen of the industry, spoke of putting 'fizz' back into the people he worked with.

Why has it grown so fast?

Since the first outplacement services in the 1960s its providers have grown and grown. The second edition of Robert Baird's *Corporate Directory of Career Change and Outplacement* identifies 120 firms operating in this expanding area of consultancy and even these are but the tip of an iceberg with a total UK market value fast approaching £50 million per annum. Outplacement has grown because the conditions supporting job security have changed and many of the changes are likely to be permanent. Knowledge of the context of job insecurity is useful in understanding the growth of outplacement and the experience of job loss.

Recession. Since the early 1970s Britain, like other European countries, has been in a recessionary phase. Following the boom of the 1950s and '60s, unemployment has been a significant and permanent feature of the employment vista. Joblessness was especially severe in the period 1979–81, with an unprecedented number of cutbacks and closures. During the 1980s the situation did not significantly change for the better, with a collapse of employment even worse than that of the pre-war slump.

Downsizing, mergers and take-overs. Economic activity in Britain has moved at an accelerating rate from manufacturing to service industries. Organizations, like empires, wax and wane but during the last twenty years restructuring has gathered momentum. The world too has become a smaller place, causing international organizations to pursue global rather than local strategies. The prospect of a single internal market in 1992 in the European Community has also brought about restructuring opportunities. In 1987 the stock market crash put many of the not so strong companies into play and liable to take-over or more amenable to merger, so a restructuring phase was quickly followed by a take-over phase, all spilling more people on to the job market.

Government policy. The early Thatcher years were marked by a refusal to support 'lame duck' industries previously shored up by government subsidy. A strong commitment to the market economy, customer choice and value for money meant many old industries going to the wall, or significant reductions in the work force as the older monolithic organizations struggled to become competitive. The government stood by and watched through non-interventionist eyes. This has been a two-edged sword for employees. On the one hand they have seen their jobs cut, on the other welfare benefits reduced, at a stroke making unemployment both real and harsh.

New employment contracts. Employment for life is no longer a concept pursued by employers, who are demanding a more flexible work force which can do more with fewer numbers. The fashionable term for this is 'leverage'. Relationships are moving from contracts of employment to contracts of service. Employers no longer want a pool of labour but rather a work force which they can hire and release at will. 'Core' and 'periphery' workers characterize these new arrangements. The smaller permanent 'core' of employees at the centre are surrounded by those on the 'periphery' who are the modern equivalent of a labour pool, unpaid during slack periods. This duality of employment is well established in Japan, and so in Britain the process is known as the 'Japanization' of employment.

New technology. 'We are expanding into smaller premises' is a common phrase in electronics. New technology makes products more reliable, services faster, administrative systems more manageable. All this means fewer employees. Whilst the early fears of the 1970s that the micro-chip and robot would destroy work have not come true, they have still released many people on to the job market and into changing career aspirations.

The net result of all this is that releasing people from organizations, changes in career and job mobility are to be expected. In all these outplacement can make a significant contribution.

The advantages of well-planned outplacement

Benefits for the organization

- Good internal and external public relations will follow from the demonstration of the organization's concern.
- The decision to release can be taken in the knowledge that the harmful effects on individuals will be mitigated or minimized.
- Compulsory redundancies can be managed more easily and cost-effectively with the practical advice of the consultancy.
- Union negotiation will be facilitated – the provision of outplacement services can tip the balance in a hard bargaining situation.
- Confrontations can be avoided and morale restored when people accept that redundancy need not mean permanent unemployment.
- The morale of those who remain will be maintained.
- A well-managed release will reduce the likelihood of key people who remain leaving at some time in the future.

Benefits for individuals

Whether executive, staff or hourly paid, people will all gain:

- Objective professional advice on strategy and self-marketing techniques.
- Better self-knowledge for career and personal life.
- Reduction in the job search time.
- Access to a network of contacts.
- More control over their future career.
- Skills which last a whole working life.

In addition, executives on a one-to-one career transition programme also have:

- Office accommodation and continuous counselling support for the duration of the job search.
- Reference library and on-line database for immediate access to company information.
- Access to unadvertised vacancies.

- Secretarial service, including printing, postage and the use of telephone and facsimile.
- Multi-country job searches through associate companies overseas.

Trade unions

There are benefits for unions too:

- Members are able to pay full subscriptions more quickly as employees get back to work.
- Less drain on union resources.
- Membership can be spread to new employers.
- Additional benefits can be won for members during the redundancy negotiations.

What outplacement will not do

Outplacement is very much a back-end activity. It will not make everything right. Many employers have provided outplacement at the end of a badly prepared and managed redundancy situation and been surprised when employees have not been grateful or morale has remained at a low ebb.

Outplacement is only part of a portfolio of options that employers need to consider if they are to be as professional and as responsible as possible in a difficult situation. Each stage should be thought through and executed with the same commitment as, say, to the development and launch of a new product or service. If the whole operation is approached with care and commitment, outplacement can make a significant contribution both to those who go and to those who stay. On its own, whilst better than nothing, it can only make a bad situation slightly better.

For this reason we start with the management of outplacement before examining how it can be delivered.

Chapter 2

Doing it right: the management of outplacement

Be prepared

Because releasing employees is difficult and usually occasioned by difficult circumstances, it is sensible to have thought the major issues through beforehand. When the redundancies are being announced is not the best time to have to wrestle with redundancy or outplacement policy. Just as disciplinary and disputes procedures are better designed, thought out and agreed before they become necessary, so too the arrangements for releasing staff should not be influenced by the contingencies of a specific situation.

In much the same way, it is wise to form preliminary relationships with outplacement consultancies so that the business of selecting one can be undertaken when there is ample time rather than during the hurly-burly of downsizing, which by its nature is always a crisis situation. No firm selects its auditors when it decides to do its end-of-year accounts. Here we are concerned not with outplacement *per se* but with how it can be avoided or what can be done to minimize redundancy. Toby Hyde, chairman of PHA, used to say to prospective clients, 'I have two wishes. First, I hope you can avoid job losses. Second, if job losses are unavoidable, I hope you will use our consultancy.'

Reducing the impact of redundancy

Redundancy is expensive in commercial as well as human terms and most employers will do all they can to ensure that it is the last option to be chosen. Many of the measures to reduce the impact are usually included in a security of employment policy or agreement whereby efforts are made to retain staff until all other reasonable options have been exhausted.

Natural wastage
This is usually the first approach. Individuals leaving because of retirement, relocation, illness or just for a better future elsewhere are not replaced. The difficulty of this approach, of course, is that it is slow and individuals are unlikely to leave those parts of the organization which need to slim down. In a recession, too, the quit rate reduces as opportunities of employment elsewhere are curtailed.

Recruitment freeze
No new appointments are made in the part of the organization affected, and wherever possible transfers are made internally. The whole emphasis changes to redeployment, and frequently redundancy policies will make this mandatory.

Overtime ban
The effect here is obvious. The work lost in overtime makes work available in normal time and thus protects head-count numbers. Such a measure is usually popular with unions but not with employees if they have been used to extended overtime working which is reflected in wages. Commercial commitments also make this option occasionally unpopular with management as with clients who have to wait longer for products.

Redeployment
Changing people's jobs to areas which are not redundant. Unfortunately people do not always have the skills required in the new positions. A firm might, for instance, find itself in the embarrassing situation of having to lay off people with mechanical skills whilst at the same time taking on employees with electronic skills. Redeployment is managed through the circulation of vacancy lists and, where possible, the offer of help with training.

Statutory requirements covering redeployment are minimal. Employers can offer suitable alternative work within the individual's period of notice. What constitutes a suitable alternative is open to debate, but if the employee refuses the new position without good reason the right to redundancy payment can be lost. What is a suitable alternative and what is a good reason for rejecting it are questions resolved through the industrial tribunal system. Having accepted an offer of an alternative, the employee enjoys a four-week trial period to see if it is suitable. The period may be extended by mutual agreement.

Relocation in the same or a suitable alternative job is also possible but the employer must ensure that the relocation demanded of the employee is reasonable. Again, in cases of conflict, this is resolved through the industrial tribunal system. Wise employers have a relocation section to cover such a contingency in their contract of employment or some other suitable document. In a dispute the facts of the situation still have to pass the test of reasonableness but relocation statements can help to tilt the balance in the employer's favour when the issue is under the scrutiny of an industrial tribunal.

Ban on temporary staff

To cope with peaks of work employers frequently take on temporary staff, either through agencies or by direct employment. When facing a redundancy situation, many firms will impose a ban on the use of such employees, thus where possible ensuring that work goes to permanent employees.

Short-time working

This is another way of preserving jobs when stocks are high and markets slow. Given that redundancy can be expensive in terms of lost skills, if an employer is confident that the market will recover in the short to medium term this is a favoured option because it is a way of maintaining skills sets and production team structures. It is still surprising how few firms have such a provision in their redundancy agreements. There are some intricate statutory rights that accrue to employees on short-time working but it is much better to have thought through this contingency beforehand and have the option available than to try and negotiate short-time working in the midst of a redundancy situation.

Other work

Many large manufacturing firms put work which they can do

themselves out to contract and in difficult times it can be pulled back in. This only pushes the redundancy problem elsewhere but for the larger firm it is another way of keeping employees together and in employment for as long as possible.

Retirement
Currently there is no legislation which forces employers to maintain the services of those over the statutory retirement age. However, because of the *Barber v. Guardian Royal Exchange* case in the European Court (May 1990) it is important that the benefits available to retirees are no different between men and women on the basis of age alone. The court's finding was:

> It is contrary to Article 49 to impose an age condition which differs according to sex in respect of pensions paid under a contracted out scheme, even if the difference in pension age for men and women is based on the one provided by the national statutory scheme.

Getting the paperwork right: the redundancy policy

It is often not realized by line management that redundancy is a form of dismissal and attracts all the same rights and privileges that accrue to unfair dismissal. Releasing individuals will in itself adversely affect the standing of the organization in the community. Appearance at a local industrial tribunal as the respondent in a case of unfair selection for redundancy will make matters worse.

A policy which provides management with the maximum flexibility is important, so that the reduced organization has a greater chance of future success. Without a policy or guidelines, then, by and large tribunals will take LIFO (Last In, First Out) to be the fairest selection process for releasing people. However, in manpower terms it could prove exceptionally difficult and expensive. The organization might have already brought in specialists to deal with a new opportunity, market or technology. They would be the last people a firm would want to release in a downsize situation but LIFO selection would demand that they be the first to go. Creed

ITT, for instance, in Brighton actively recruited staff with electronic as well as mechanical skills because of rapid changes in the market, requiring more electronic components. In such a case long-serving employees with only mechanical skills would be the more appropriate people to release, as opposed to the more recent recruits. Or, to take another example, it would be inappropriate to release an employee with a perfect attendance record over the last three years instead of one with five years' service whose attendance record was abysmal. The existence of a policy guides management over such difficulties.

No organization can guarantee continuous employment these days, so it is good practice to develop a redundancy policy before the need arises. If redundancies are declared a week after the policy is agreed an employer will have a hard time convincing a tribunal that it was not written to prevent the individuals in question from claiming that they were specifically selected.

Goodyear Tyre & Rubber Company, mentioned earlier, is an American multinational with a large manufacturing base in Wolverhampton, and is the major employer in the locality. Goodyear's redundancy policy represents a good working document. It sets out measures to reduce redundancy, and explains the consultation arrangements and selection criteria, all issues better thought through in advance. It is reproduced in Appendix 1 on page 142. (Other examples of redundancy policies can be found in Income Data Services study No. 442, December 1988, and others as they become available.)

Personality characteristics of executives selected for redundancy

Company policy is not the only factor in the decision as to who goes. There are 'below the line' issues as well. All experienced HR managers know that line managers will do their utmost to release those they would like to see go, irrespective of policy considerations. This is known as the 'brown-eyed boy list' but there are some interesting psychological factors in how managers select their colleagues and subordinates for redundancy.

An interesting study was undertaken in 1986 by Cranfield School of Management and the Forty Plus Research Fund (a charity associated with the outplacement consultancy Pauline Hyde & Associates). The research posed the question 'In a partial redundancy situation where some employees are selected to go, is there a personality type which is more vulnerable?' In other words, do certain executives survive in organizations and others go partly because of their disposition, on the basis of personality factors? The consultancy provided results of a 16PF personality questionnaire of 204 executives who had been outplaced and their scores were compared first to 178 business executives and secondly to a group of 855 managers and technical specialists who had applied to a British electronics manufacturing company.

After examining the mean scores of the redundant executives against the management population, a significant profile emerged. The redundant managers were:

- More calm.
- Socially more bold, uninhibited.
- Much more imaginative and unconventional.
- Less shrewd, more natural and forthright.
- Less self-critical.
- Less tense and overwrought.

Thus, the research suggested, 'It is those executives whose "N" factor profile indicates a lack of "political" skills who are likely to be redundant, compared with other executives.' Typically, then, it is the 'grey people' who stay but the more independently minded, conscientious, imaginative and unconventional who are likely to be released.

An interesting inference can be drawn from this finding. Firstly, should the organization get into difficulty, beware of releasing the more creative element of your executive cadre. Secondly, redundant executives can possess very useful characteristics for organizations that need creativity, imagination and forthrightness to manage their current and future environments.

Payment arrangements for releasing staff

In addition to the minimum statutory payments it is now common for organizations to provide additional separation payments or compensation. The reasons are twofold. First, to maintain the employer's reputation in the job market. Even in times of downsizing and recession employers will still need to recruit key staff and consequently money spent maintaining the company's recruitment reputation is cash well spent. Marks & Spencer, knowing that it would have to return to the recruitment pool and wanting to maintain its recruitment reputation, made significant payments to junior supervisors on releasing them in 1991. The company even did the same for graduates who had been offered a traineeship after their degree exams which, in the event, could not be confirmed.

But there is another reason. Additional payments in such a situation are the acceptable face of capitalism. Good employers are deeply concerned that they are unable to maintain the implied assumption in the employment contract that employment is continuous. Organizations offer employees more than a legal relationship built around the concept of master and servant, and there is a real desire to assist those who have given good service and – usually through no fault of their own – find their job disappearing. Additional payments in such situations can be considered tangible evidence of the employer's social responsibility.

On the other hand, additional payments can be used to lock the employees in until it is convenient for the firm to release them. In a large-scale rundown over an extended period employees who are to be released later rather than earlier not unnaturally become concerned that all the jobs in the neighbourhood will be taken up by those released in the earlier stages. Outplacement consultants know that jobs are not unlike tins on a supermarket shelf: they are continually being replenished – by natural wastage, retirement, start-ups and organizational growth. Employees, however, because of their lack of knowledge, think that each time a colleague gets a job there is one less in a finite pool. When the news of redundancy has broken, employees look to their own long-term interests. When they are offered a job during the run-down period, not surprisingly they want to leave and get on with the new job without loss of separation payments.

The Redundancy Payments Act 1965 (which was largely incorporated into the Employment Protection (Consolidation) Act 1978) gives to most employees who have completed two or more years' full-time employment a lump sum when dismissed for redundancy. This is calculated on an age-length of service-week's pay formula. The payment is tax free and is an entitlement of the employee which can not normally be taken away.

Perhaps the most helpful guidelines on the principles and purpose of the Redundancy Payments Act was delivered by the President of the Industrial Tribunals of England and Wales in the case of *Wynes v Southrepps Hall Broiler Farm Ltd*, who summed it up by saying:

> 'It has been suggested that a redundancy payment is not a golden handshake, but was intended to tide a man over the period of unemployment, and that when he has no employment it is unfair and wrong that he should get a redundancy payment. The policy behind redundancy payment is not that it should tide a worker over a period of unemployment – earnings-related benefits are instructed for that purpose.
>
> The stated purpose of the redundancy payments scheme is twofold: it is to compensate for loss of security and to encourage workers to accept redundancy without damaging industrial relations. A redundancy payment is compensation for the loss of a right which a long term employee has in his job. Just as a property owner has right in his property and when he is deprived he is entitled to compensation, so a long term employee is considered to have a right analogous to a property right in his job: he has a right to security and his rights gain value with the years . . . the purpose of redundancy pay is to compensate a worker for loss of a job, irrespective of whether that loss leads to unemployment. It is to compensate him for loss of security, possible loss of earnings and fringe benefits, and the uncertainty and anxiety of job change . . . There is a distinction between the compensation for loss of office and the relief of hardship'
>
> *Industrial Tribunal Review* 1968, 407, p. 407ff

The week's pay was based upon what was then thought to be the average manual take-home payment and since its introduction, it has been reviewed regularly, usually in the spring of each year. This may have been a reasonably generous payment in the early 1960s, but is not a significant sum when compared to the average take-home pay in the UK today. This has led to the practice by employers of giving additional payments to encourage the employee to stay to the end of the notice period or until the firm is ready to release him or her. For example, a key skilled employee aged 26 with five years' service may not feel that four or five weeks of the statutory maximum – his entitlement under the redundancy payment scheme – is not worth waiting for and leave early, causing considerable difficulty to the employer. Additional payments, conditional on good service up to the specified release date, are a way of encouraging people to stay.

Some firms not only give extra on top of the redundancy payments but also make an additional payment called a loyalty bonus. For instance, a week's gross pay may be due for each week served of the official thirteen-week period of notice. But it is only earned if the employee stays to the end. Thus it is that separation payments may have three components: redundancy entitlement, separation payment, loyalty payment. Given that it cuts both ways, and that when employees secure a job only to see it go to someone else because they cannot start yet, they can become frustrated and aggrieved, outplacement consultants can be particularly useful in explaining how the job market works and the continuing availability of jobs.

In appropriate circumstances pay may be given in lieu of notice, and this, of course, can be regarded as an additional benefit rather than compensation for the loss of formal notice.

Separation or severance pay has considerable implications for the provision and start time of outplacement services, particularly job shops and resource centres, and this question is examined in the section on the timing of outplacement.

Principles of separation payments

As early as 1981 the Institute of Manpower Studies at Sussex University surveyed arrangements for redundant employees and the principles it discovered are still valid today:

1 The more senior you are in the organization, the more generous the additional payment.
2 The longer your service, the greater the additional payment.
3 The older you are at the time of the redundancy, the greater your additional payment.
4 Voluntary separations received greater additional payment.

Principles 2 and 3, of course, are also enshrined in the Redundancy Payments Act provisions. The practice of giving additional payments has grown considerably since the 1981 study, partly through the normal phenomenon of large organizations following good working practice as regards terms and conditions for executives and partly through collective bargaining arrangements for junior and hourly paid staff.

Payments vary from sector to sector and from firm to firm, generally reflecting the remuneration levels in that sector. So, for instance, oil companies give more than engineering firms, which in turn are more generous than the public sector. A representative selection of the terms made available by large companies as at mid-1990 is listed at the end of this section. Outplacement consultancies can usually advise on the size of payment that is the 'going rate' for the industry and sometimes for the locality. Additional payments are currently highest in the South East, followed by the Midlands and North West. Firms in the South West are reputed to be the least generous.

When senior executives were released from Rediffusion, a high-tech engineering firm in Sussex, during its 1991 reorganization, one of their main concerns was not just the content and size of their separation package but how the package compared with the rest of the industry. Just as individuals expect parity in the matter of pay and benefits, the same principle applies to separation arrangements, especially as those released are frequently angry about their loss and look for ways of venting their feelings of disappointment. It is better to have all such arrangements made long before (and reviewed regularly) than face the unpleasantness of negotiation, sometimes through solicitors, with released employees or executives for an improved separation package.

Selected severance payments

Unless stated otherwise, all payments are inclusive of statutory entitlements. (From IDS Study No. 464, August 1990, reprinted by permission. IDS regularly publish these and other useful pay data.)

BREL. Statutory payments, plus supplementary payments of one week's pay per year of service over fifteen years, or after age 45 whichever is longer, and in addition an amount equal to 40 per cent of the total payment. Also, employees aged less than 50: two weeks' pay for each of the first ten years and one week's pay for each of the next ten years; employees aged 50 or more: two weeks' pay for each year of potential employment up to retirement age.

Blakeborough Valves. Statutory terms plus an *ex gratia* payment of £3.50 per year.

Boots the Chemist. Per year of service: under age 41, two weeks' pay; after age 41, two and a half weeks' pay.

British Coal. Per year of service: three weeks' pay, plus supplementary lump-sum payments ranging from £2,500 under age 21 to £10,000 at 30 years and over. Maximum payment: thirty years' service at a maximum of £300 per week.

British Steel (Teesside). Statutory payments, plus *ex gratia* payments as follows: two to four years' service, ten weeks' pay; five to nine years, fifteen weeks' pay; ten years and over, twenty-three weeks' pay.

Co-operative Wholesale Society. Statutory payments calculated without reference to the earnings limit, increased by 50 per cent to nearest half-week. Minimum payment: two weeks' pay.

Carnation Foods. Per year of service: up to age 40, three weeks' pay; age 40 up to 55, four weeks' pay; age 55 to retirement, five weeks' pay. Minimum payment: three weeks' pay (six weeks' after twelve months' service).

Clark's Shoes. Per year of service: 1.75 × basic pay plus a supplement of three to twelve weeks' pay for workers aged 50–4 and not immediately eligible for a pension. Maximum payment: 65 to 40 weeks' pay at age 55 and over.

MSF terms – per year of service: two weeks' salary, plus supplementary payments ranging from £2,525 to £525 for workers aged 50–4. Maximum payment: sixty-five weeks (sixty-three to thirty if within ten years of retirement).

Continental Can. Double the statutory payments, without the earnings limit. Minimum payment: four weeks' basic pay. Maximum payment: relates to twenty years' service.

Ferranti International. Statutory payments plus a company severance payment: hourly paid, four weeks' basic wage; staff, one month's basic salary. Also service-based severance pay: one week's pay × ¾ × years of service (maximum twelve weeks' pay).

Ind Coope Burton Brewery. Per year of service: three and a half weeks' pay. Minimum payment: fifteen weeks' pay. Maximum payment: relates to forty years' service and must not exceed £29,000.

Landis & Gyr. Manual workers: statutory payments plus 50 per cent and an additional quarter of a week's pay for each year over age 20.

Nationwide Anglia. Per year of total service: age up to 25, three weeks' pay; age 25 to 35, three and three-quarter weeks' pay; age 36 to 45, four and a half weeks' pay; age 46 to 55, six weeks' pay; over age 55, seven and a half weeks' pay. Maximum payment: two years' pay.

Tesco. Statutory payments plus an additional service entitlement ranging from eight weeks' pay with one month's service but under five years', to fifty-two weeks' pay with twenty-five years' service or more.

Planning ahead: the outplacement policy

Just as organizations find it makes sense to have a redundancy policy, an outplacement policy is also useful. Besides the obvious reasons, a policy is helpful when different HR managers at different locations have responsibility for releases, as the policy can ensure parity across the organization. Released individuals quickly find out what others in a similar situation have received and, not unnaturally, want an equivalent deal. Some are sure to find out what is the 'going rate' for the industry or sector and demand it.

The major components of a policy could include some or all of the following:

Reason for the policy
This states the desire of the organization to help individuals who are released and its intention of fulfilling the role of a good employer who is concerned about the people released.

Commitment to continued employment
No responsible employers willingly take staff on and train them only to release them later. Nor will they casually hire and fire. All good employers offer the incentive of permanent employment unless they explicitly state the contrary at the beginning of the employment by means of a service contract. Just as the employer hopes each employee will behave well yet lays down a disciplinary procedure, so the employer will outplace individuals only as a last resort, and the policy should bear witness to the fact.

Relation to other policies and procedures
Outplacement is not normally allowed to those who are disciplined and leave the organization on account of poor conduct, incapability or some other substantial reason, and this should be made clear. A member of staff who is promoted in good faith on both sides but who subsequently fails and is taken through the disciplinary route would still not normally qualify for outplacement. Nor is outplacement normally provided when an individual is dismissed, although more and more executives are having an outplacement provision built into their contract of employment, irrespective of the manner in which they leave the organization.

Where an organization has a remuneration and benefit policy there should be a link to the outplacement policy and payment arrangements.

Circumstances when outplacement is provided
Usually outplacement is provided when the job loss is through no fault of the employee, whether it be due to economies of scale, structural changes or whatever, through to the situation where an employee is unable to relocate.

How employees qualify for outplacement
Some employers put a service qualification on the provision of outplacement of so many months' or years' employment.

Redundancy payments are not triggered until two years of service, and this has been used as an indicator when individuals are released. In mass redundancy situations a service qualification is not normally used because it is taken to be devisive. Other employers have not given outplacement support to employees reaching retirement but have given them a cash sum in lieu, on the basis that this is more appropriate to their particular situation or have provided them with retirement counselling.

Who authorizes the provision of outplacement?
This is most useful in complicated organizational structures because it also ensures that all released individuals receive the same level of service (see below). It is also helpful for the outplacement counselling to have one port of call for the administration of invoices and for the organization to have control of expenditure. This latter point is important when large outplacement contracts can run into hundreds of thousands of pounds.

Who administers outplacement?
In downsizing there is always a large administration requirement – organizing resources for job shops and rooms for seminars, etc. – so a nominated administrator is useful. In a plant with 1,000 people, such matters as which employees attend which programmes when, can keep a personnel officer and a secretary busy almost full-time for the duration of the programme.

So that billing arrangements can be verified strict records need to be kept of who has had what service and when. During a downsizing employees are very keen to get as much out of the outplacement service as they can, and when a variety of different types of service are being provided it is very important that the employer controls who gets what. Otherwise, not surprisingly, individuals will engineer themselves into the most expensive help they can – and the outplacement consultancy will be only too pleased to provide it!

Who evaluates outplacement support?
Outplacement is not inexpensive. At the end of one project it was estimated that twenty-five personnel manager *years* had

been devoted to it, and questions were rightly asked about value for money. There is a real temptation for executives to turn the downsizing over to the consultancy and then get on with the many requirements of the new organization. Evaluation is important not only because good stewardship requires it but as a way of ensuring that the consultancy continues to give good service. It is on the basis of good performance that future outplacement contracts should be awarded, and this can only be done through evaluation.

Types of outplacement support and eligibility

Just as different benefits are given at different levels in the organization, so it is appropriate for different types of outplacement support to be given. The job loss can be just as traumatic for a teaperson as for the chairperson. However, their job search arrangements are different and warrant different types of service. Types of outplacement services are outlined elsewhere, but the basis is one-to-one counselling for executives and group training for less senior staff.

What is important is to be able to justify different types of service and support in objective terms. At GTE, ABB or Marks & Spencer, for example, a certain grade or salary level would trigger a certain type of service. At Trebor, the confectionery people, there was an interesting variant arrangement where a formula took into account not only salary but also age and length of service. It worked out the basis that a 50 year old on the same salary as a 30 year old would need more support in pursuing the next career stage.

Outplacement support cannot be cashed in

Most people being released are encountering outplacement services for the first time in their career. Some people are so angry with the firm that they refuse everything on offer, even outplacement. Some, not having experienced outplacement before, if given a choice would much rather have the cash value of the service added to their separation package. Organizations are well advised *not* to offer the choice of outplacement or an enhanced separation package, since most people will opt for the latter out of ignorance of the benefits of the former. Since most participants who go through outplacement get a job sooner, and with an enhanced remuneration package, outplacement fees represent good value, both to the individual and to the releasing employer.

Computation of the separation package

Most firms these days make payments over and above the statutory minimum. This is especially so for senior staff and executives. Multiples of earnings based on service or statistics, or sometimes both, can be set out so that employees know what they can expect to receive.

Computation of benefits

For executives with a significant proportion of benefits in their total package many organizations allow the use of the benefits after separation – for example, use of the company car for six months or until a new position is achieved, whichever is sooner. Sometimes medical, life insurance and pension provision is made available to the departing executive on the same basis. The advantage to the released executive is enormous, because his or her lifestyle is cut back gradually rather than everything going at once. If the cars are owned rather than leased, allowing the executive to purchase the car at book price can even save the organization the problem of disposal. The extension of health cover is particularly useful. The shock of dismissal is not infrequently associated subsequently with increased susceptibility to illness. So this form of cover is particularly welcome.

The provision of financial advice

Separation packages for executives can be quite considerable and for most people represent the largest single lump sum they will ever receive in their life. It is rumoured that on the day Caterpillar closed at Uddingston, in 1987, millions of pounds were paid out, attracting a great deal of interest in the financial services and consumer durable sectors. At such a time individuals need quality, independent advice built around their own particular needs and medium- and long-term aspirations.

If individuals work their notice it is not uncommon for a firm to have a nominated and qualified professional on site to give advice. For executives, some firms will provide a set number of hours of financial guidance with a professional adviser. Anyone who requires additional support and advice can fund it themselves. It is usual to offer employees the names of two firms of advisers and let them choose.

The policy statement outlines what the firm will support, who the nominated advisers are and how access is to be arranged. A disclaimer is sometimes added to the effect that individuals are responsible for the advice they choose to take.

Nominated supplier of outplacement services

Just as the organization vets and nominates financial advisers, so the providers of outplacement can be vetted and nominated. There are two major schools of thought here. Some employers like to nominate as many as three consultancies, so that the individual executive can choose which one to work with. This means that the individual can select the consultancy and the counsellor with whom he or she feels most comfortable. Consultancies, of course, much prefer to be the sole supplier of the services, for obvious commercial reasons, but they do make the valid point that someone who has just been released and is in job loss trauma is not in the best state to make a choice.

Some firms have different consultancies to provide services at various levels of status or grades. The reasons are legion but the main one is that key senior executives are sensitive about sharing the same resources or counselling facilities as more junior staff. Sometimes the reverse is true too. The major providers of outplacement services themselves tend to have expertise in dealing with particular grades of employee. Sanders and Sidney, for instance, based in Piccadilly, have an excellent reputation for dealing with the most senior of executives. Focus, run by Bridget Litchfield and based in Barnet, is known for its good work with large groups. Each consultancy began from a particular niche but can now service the total spectrum. Wright Associates reckon to deal with executives worldwide because of their international network of offices. Human resource directors need to familiarize themselves with what the market can provide and develop a suitable association with one or two providers.

Precedent disclaimer

There is always an odd trickle of people being released from big firms, and in such circumstances the organization can be quite generous in its separation package. Should the tide of fortune change, with the organization facing the prospect of large-scale redundancies, it may not be able to afford to be so generous. There needs to be a statement to the effect that the company may and if necessary will make changes to its outplacement provisions from time to time in the light of circumstances.

Selection of an outplacement consultancy

From just three outplacement agencies in the mid-1970s the number had grown to some forty by the mid-'80s and now almost every consultancy claims it can provide such services. Outplacement has mushroomed in the UK, much as recruitment agencies did in the 1950s and early '60s, partly as a result of market need but also because it is potentially profitable, with fees at the top end about 15 per cent of leaving salary plus an administration fee of anything up to £6,000. Even when dealing with hourly paid personnel an outplacement contract can be quite sizeable, with a value of up to £500,000, to provide support for a major downsizing where thousands of employees are made redundant.

Organizations are organic by nature. They continually grow and shrink, merge or become an acquisition, and in all these situations outplacement is required. Even in growth situations managers sometimes cannot grow with the firm and have to be let go. The computer industry is a good example. A small entrepreneurial firm staffed by technocrats suddenly finds that it is a large firm in need of professional management because of the difficulties left by the 'techies'. Thus in the personnel world where there is constant need and high fee-earning potential the HR director can expect to be inundated by outplacement consultancies offering their services. How the choice is best made is the subject of this section.

Outplacement is no different from other consultancy and the best initial selection is made on recommendation from HR colleagues, and the IPM Personnel Consultancy Assignment Service can advise on IPM-qualified members practising outplacement. The major decisions would seem to involve the types of service required, the numbers being released and the likely status or level of the released individuals. The original consultancies began and gained their experience by servicing top executives and are particularly good in that area. Other consultancies have specialized in shopfloor and clerical staff from the start. Today all the large consultancies have moved up or down the organizational tree and can cater for all levels of personnel.

Later on the scene were the large accountancy firms which have set up an outplacement division providing services not merely for their own clients but any firm releasing staff. Some of the larger organizations, such as British Coal, have set up outplacement facilities of their own which will also service clients outside the parent organization. Finally there are outplacement consultancies which specialize in a specific sector such as banking, computing or the pharmaceutical industry.

In selecting a consultancy some of the issues that could usefully be considered are as follows:

How long has it been in business?

Anyone can win a contract once, but the length of time a firm has been in business is a significant indicator of the reliability and quality of its services. Outplacement consultants are rather like managers of football teams in that they are only as good as their last match. Repeat business is dependent on continual success.

What is its main sector experience?

If yours is a computer firm and the outplacement consultancy has most of its experience in, say, banking or oil, it will be able to provide some support but it will be using your released employees to move up its own learning curve. Someone from manufacturing can be helped by a firm with good experience in pharmaceuticals because the outplacement process is essentially the same whatever the background of the client. However, you would be better served by a firm with direct experience of your industry. All consultancies will, of course, claim expertise, but just as the wise accountant takes out a credit check so the wise HR executive would do well to check a consultancy's background.

What level of personnel has it experience of dealing with?
If you are releasing an executive earning £100,000 per annum plus all the add-ons you will want to make sure that the consultancy's facilities and counsellors will enjoy credibility with your nominee. This is not to say that an ex-apprentice supervisor trained in counselling skills who has been in outplacement consultancy for years cannot give solid advice to a recently released regional manager of a large financial institution. But time is inevitably taken up in establishing his credibility. For the same reasons you would not want an ex-banker trained in counselling working with a redundant toolroom fitter.

What are the resources on offer?
This is particularly relevant to the one-to-one or executive counselling programme where a consultancy offers a 'home from home' or a place from which the released executive can work. Here there is tremendous variation in the facilities provided. For 15 per cent of final exit salary plus an administration fee the following facilities and resources could reasonably be anticipated:

- Desk or office to work from.
- Telephone and fax.
- Mail out facilities.
- Secretarial support.
- Word-processing and desk-top publishing.
- Journals, newspapers and trade magazines.
- Major directories, including *Kompass* and Kelly's.
- Sector profiles such as Jordan's reports.
- Headhunter lists.
- Use of an electronic database such as Textline.
- Access to a counsellor.
- Meeting with a chartered psychologist or a qualified career adviser.
- A personal computer available with appropriate software.
- Referral to an independent financial adviser who is a member of FIMBRA and the IFAP.

For some organizations the location of the office has a bearing on the selection of a consultancy.

What calibre are the counsellors and how qualified are they?
This is a very significant area, equally applicable in the case of one-to-one or group contracts alike. In the one-to-one, as mentioned, it is important for the counsellor to establish credibility as well as rapport with the person he or she is working with. The better agencies will have consultants not only trained in counselling skills but who have held senior line positions as well. There is also the 'grey factor' to be considered. Older executives find it inappropriate to be counselled by someone twenty years their junior, however competent the person may be. The availability of a female counsellor is also important. Some women executives prefer a female counsellor, whereas it is not usually an issue for men.

Should part of the process include psychological assessment, the consultancy ought to employ or be able to refer clients to a chartered psychologist who is also a registered test user. Redundant executives are, not unnaturally, under a great deal of stress, and it is important for the significant contribution psychometrics can make to be handled by a professional. Just as important, career counsellors should have a qualification recognized by the British Association of Counselling. This is not to say that good advice cannot be given by a wise and sympathetic older manager, but it is no substitute for professionalism in this important skill area. In making the choice of the consultancy the HR director should meet and vet the people who will be counselling his or her nominees.

What exactly is being provided?
Since each outplacement project is different in some way or other, it is important to know exactly what is to be provided and how, when and by whom. Some consultancies provide support on an open-ended basis, some provide it over a specified period of weeks or months, and some provide assistance on a session basis. Some give unlimited mailshot support and produce as many of the candidates' CVs as necessary; others are quite specific in what they will provide. The better consultancies provide psychometrics, financial guidance and advice on dress and appearance as standard. For others these are extra and have to be paid for by the company or the individual. Training by means of closed-circuit television may be provided for some group sessions but not others. Not only

is it good management practice to know exactly what is being provided, it is also necessary for company fee structures and for post-project evaluation. The actual recipient of the outplacement, too, needs to know what to expect from the service on offer.

How is success evaluated?
This is not simply a matter of seeing that those affected get a job. Factors such as average time to place and the standard deviation for time taken are useful in ensuring that realistic expectations can be held out to prospective clients. A number of questions can be asked.

Through which avenues were the jobs achieved? Many consultancies claim to have huge banks of unadvertised jobs. In that case the placement rate through channels other than advertisements or agencies should support the claim. How do the candidates' new remuneration packages compare with their last job? In an executive one-to-one service it should not be unreasonable to expect that in over half the cases the new job should be paying more than the previous one.

Where job shops or advice centres are set up, statistics should be readily available on such things as:

- Number of organizations contacted.
- Number of vacancies identified.
- Number of interviews arranged.
- Number of offers secured.
- Number of positions secured.

Evidence of these types of statistics for previous contracts should be readily available.

One unscrupulous consultancy with little experience claimed that it could not provide such information because it was 'too confidential'. The truth was that it had never run job shops before. The wise HR director asked for proof from the firm's accountants as independent auditors. He did not need to know the details, only enough to verify the claim. If the consultancy cannot tell the client what measures of success it uses, then the project is highly unlikely to come up to expectations.

Has it got professional indemnity? Has it ever had to use it?
Giving career and psychological advice to individuals who are stressed and anxious needs to be done in the most professional manner. If things go wrong the HR director will want to be assured that it will not be his or her firm that is sued for incompetence. On the larger contracts have the independent self-employed trainers and counsellors individual professional liability cover?

What advice can it give outside the outplacement itself?
Will the consultancy train the client's managers in how to release their employees in the best possible way yet ensure that all the statutory requirements have been satisfied? The better consultancies provide such support at nominal cost, sometimes without charge, because the better the local management handle this aspect of the redundancy the easier it makes the job of the outplacement consultancy working with the people released.

What is the ratio of consultants to clients or participants?
Any outplacement consultancy can have a register of counsellors, but the essential question is how many clients they are dealing with individually. As a rule of thumb for one-to-one work, much more than one counsellor to an active list of thirty-five people and the executive outplacement service begins to suffer from quality dilution. Clients find they cannot get to see their counsellor, and counsellors begin to suffer from fatigue and burn-out.

Who counsels the counsellors might also be a useful subsidiary question. What professional build-up or support arrangements are on hand for those operating at the emotionally draining interface of continuous counselling? The first week of a job shop or advice centre opening requires about one counsellor to fifty people, because the initial interest is so high. Thereafter one consultant per hundred released employees, if they are all on the same site, is more than adequate.

What relations are there with other professional groups?
Career moves throw up all kinds of different needs, and the better consultancy should have a proven network of professional and other people to whom referrals can be made. The

obvious category, of course, is the headhunting fraternity, with whom one would expect very close relations for the obvious reasons. Other groups could include (in no particular order): colour adviser, for dress and style; clinical psychologist, for personal or domestic difficulties; financial adviser – and, of course, the network of previous clients who can advise the recently unemployed on contacts and openings in a particular sector.

Measuring success

Purchasers of outplacement should ask themselves, 'What do I want to get out of this project?' and 'How will I know it has been successful?' Outplacement, like PR, is essentially a 'soft' service. It is difficult to quantify success, yet if management are committing tens if not hundreds of thousands of pounds to a project it is important to set criteria for expectations, measuring quality and evaluating success. Below are some suggestions which could form the basis of discussion.

Hard measures

They are called 'hard' because figures from the before, during and after stages of a downsizing can be collated and compared.

- Over 50 per cent of those released in new jobs within twelve weeks of leaving work.
- Over 80 per cent of those released in new jobs within twenty-four weeks of leaving work.
- Over 50 per cent of those with new jobs in positions with a better total remuneration package than the original post.
- Absenteeism for three months after the downsizing at the same level as before.
- Turnover for twelve months after the downsizing at the same level as before.
- No claims for unfair selection for redundancy to an industrial tribunal or suit for wrongful dismissal in the county or High Court.
- No increase in the level of accidents during the period of notice of redundancy.
- No increase in the level of employee theft or seepage during the notice of redundancy period.

- Level of applications for jobs from the locality remains unchanged.
- Industrial relations activity decreases or remains the same for six months after the downsizing.
- Similar or increased productivity level for three months after the downsizing.

Soft measures
They are called 'soft' because they are difficult to measure and reflect people's perceptions.

- Similar or higher levels of morale after the downsizing.
- No marked difference in working relationships at an individual, departmental or inter-office level.
- Minimal recriminations. The majority of people affected feel the company acted as fairly as it could in the circumstances.
- Discussions weighted more towards future opportunities than past glories.
- General willingness to try new things and be more positive about change.
- Commitment to clients and quality remains the same.
- Management statements and declarations of intent are trusted.
- The downsizing event felt to have been well handled, considering the circumstances.
- For most of the time communications are thought to have been good.
- The organization is regarded as a good place to work for in terms of both career and atmosphere.

Selection of consultants for group work

The choice of consultants for groups is just as important as for one-to-one counselling. Most outplacement concerns have a small team of trainers and when they win a large contract they hire independent self-employed consultants. The latter now represent quite an extensive band of people, and if the placers of large outplacement contracts sift through the lists of associates they will see the same names recurring under the banner of a variety of consultancies. As one member of the

Coal Board was heard to say, 'It doesn't seem to matter who we give the outplacement contract to. We'll get the same consultants working on it whoever we choose!'

The calibre of the consultants or trainers in any outplacement project is paramount. Where group work is concerned it would be wise for the HR manager or a nominee to meet the trainers who are going to work with the people to be released. Besides probing their training and counselling skills, questions should be asked such as:

- Will this person be credible with my people?
- Has he or she personal knowledge of the industry?
- Has this person worked successfully before with groups similar to my people at this grade?
- Does this person come across as confident and free of personal problems?
- Can this person work at an individual as well as group level?

The fourth point is important because many people, particularly from training and personnel, who have lost their jobs are attracted to outplacement counselling and may still be going through their own job loss transition. Their skills, knowledge and experience are obviously right for outplacement consultancy but their emotional state makes them unsuitable. Being in the same situation as those you are working with is not empathy; too often a trainer in this position will look to the participant for mutual support. The significance of the last question is that whilst the bulk of the process may be in groups it will be necessary for the trainer to identify individual agendas and change from a training approach to one more appropriate to counselling.

One of the areas where group work differs in its nature from one-to-one counselling is the expression of anger. Of course there is anger in the individual situation, but in groups participants feel less obliged to restrain their feelings. One of the reasons why programmes of less than a day are not recommended is that groups not infrequently spend anything up to half a day giving vent to their anger at the organization which has released them. The reasons are examined in the section on responses to job loss. It is essential that counsellors have the skill to deal with this.

The principle is, then, that all counsellors or trainers employed on the outplacement project should have their biography available for scrutiny and be interviewed to ensure suitability. When the organization's interests and those of its former employees are at stake nothing can be taken for granted. It is not unknown for an outplacement agency to win a contract only to go straight to the local job centre looking for would-be counsellors to train.

Other questions

In addition to these topics the normal questions that one would ask of any consultancy should not be forgotten, such as:

- What makes your service unique?
- Why should we select you?
- What have been your most recent successes?
- What market niche do you aim at?
- What are your particular strengths?
- How do I raise reservations about the service should there be any?
- Which clients have you lost in the last twelve months?
- How do we negotiate on price?

Consulting the unions

Although not necessary, it can be helpful to all concerned if the outplacement consultancy meets the trade unions should the people being released be members of a recognized union. Apart from any considerations of good industrial relations the stewards have their own effective networks which can check on the consultancy being used. They provide management with a quality and sanity check if the services are not up to expectation. In redundancy situations employees will frequently ask their steward or their representative whether or not they should attend the programmes being laid on. It is obviously reassuring if the reply is that the steward has met the outplacement providers and can speak from personal knowledge.

Sometimes, however, support from the unions is not forthcoming, especially if they are fighting the closure and recommending members not to accept the redundancy. Even in these circumstances, it is still wise to offer a meeting. Union representatives have sat down with the outplacement consultants in many difficult situations. As one steward put it, 'Whatever happens, we want our members working for someone. You can't represent them if they haven't got jobs.'

There are usually three main things on the union agenda if a meeting can be arranged. The first is usually how the package rates and what other employers are giving. Surprising as it may seem, there is a market 'rate' for release packages but an outplacement consultancy, for obvious reasons, would be unwise to comment. Trade unionists should know that they can get advice from their own excellent information base, the Labour Research Department in London. The second is usually a request for no pre-selection of employees. That is to say, if local employers ring the plant that is closing to say they have vacancies, e.g. for three electricians, the releasing employer will not be pressured into naming only those who do the job best, or have a good attendance record, or are not troublemakers, etc. The unions demand that all those who qualify as electricians, irrespective of their history with the company, should be nominated. To my mind the request is quite justified. Unsympathetic managers, who may themselves be on the job market, are prone to the strange view that they should determine who goes forward for interview and who does not. Even more unscrupulous are those who try to settle old scores by deliberately interfering with the future career opportunities of their subordinates.

The other main concern of the unions is confidentiality of information concerning their members. It may be, for instance, that an individual has been moonlighting for a considerable period, or that someone has lied about his or her age, qualifications or domestic circumstances, or that a medical condition has been kept from the employer. Such matters become particularly sensitive in a close-down when released employees are in competition for jobs elsewhere within the organization.

The unions can also help in terms of information on jobs and job opportunities. The local trades council can be as effective as the local employers' federation when it comes to information on who is hiring whom. My experience is that union communications on matters of employment are far superior to those of employers. When releasing large numbers of union members it is sensible to invite a full-time official – with local management permission, of course – to address them on their union status during unemployment and the support they can expect from their branch or section.

When to do what: the timing

The timing of outplacement services is crucial, especially when the employer wishes to retain staff to a specified future date because of a phased close-down, stock build or some other reason. Essentially it is a balancing act between wanting to be seen to provide help on the one hand and not wanting people to get another job too soon. Outplacement is frequently provided in circumstances where the management want to 'hold on' to employees as long as possible for operational reasons. The message here is 'Look, don't panic and leave us early, because we'll provide job search support.' In such a situation the timing is of the essence, because once the outplacement begins employees will find jobs quickly. If the timing is not right the employer could end up in the worst of all worlds – paying for the consultancy, losing employees early and having to manage disgruntled ones with jobs to go to but locked into a completion bonus scheme.

Obviously the outplacement consultancy is well positioned to advise in such a situation. A possible strategy could be as follows. As soon as the closure is announced the consultancy meets those affected to tell them about the services that will be provided, how the job shop and/or training will be organized and in factual terms what results can reasonably be expected, given the location, industry and time of year. This does not merely inform the employees but is interpreted as a public commitment from their employer to provide tangible assistance. The next stage is to identify an area for the resource centre and have Internal Maintenance involved in cleaning it out, redecoration, putting up large notice boards, setting up telephones and installing furniture. This again is a positive sign that help is on the way.

Since the average time for hourly paid and junior staff to find work is around eight weeks (for senior managers it is twelve weeks and for those over fifty it is sixteen weeks), outplacement training and job shop activity should ideally commence any time in the last eight weeks before the release date. It should be remembered, however, that it does take about two weeks to get the job shop set up and for it to find a sufficient number of vacancies. It really destroys the credibility of the operation if employees turn up at the job shop on the first day the consultants and the telephone job searchers arrive and find a centre without a job in it. It is essential to allow time to get a good batch of vacancies in so that on the first day – when everyone visits the job shop – even those who are not leaving are impressed with the potential it offers their less fortunate colleagues.

Outplacement training can begin some eight weeks before the agreed release date, provided management are happy to release staff for interviews with prospective employers. Job shop counsellors are usually good at persuading local employers to keep vacancies open until the Monday after the official leaving date, and, of course, this is ideal where people leave on the Friday and start the new job the following Monday. This is possible when the job shop has an eight-week run in areas of high employment. About 85 per cent placement was achieved in this way for hourly paid personnel at Duracell in Crawley, Sussex. The figure was perhaps exceptional because Crawley/Gatwick is unusual in its continued economic growth during the recession, being in the South East and near a fast-growing international airport, but it nevertheless shows what is possible.

Contingency planning

Even if management have done well in keeping the news of impending redundancies secret, employees usually have an inkling that something is up. In a merger it is obvious to all that economies of scale are one of the main attractions. But in other situations there are tell-tale signs. Employees know when business is poor as overtime reduces or there is a recruitment freeze. No one has to be a genius to appreciate that stock moving slowly from the store means business is down. Other strange things begin to happen. Key equipment is moved to other plants when it really does not make sense if business is normal.

For the ordinary employee the pace of the organization is simply different. Senior managers too begin to behave differently before a redundancy. Desks which were once left untidy are suddenly bare of papers at night; offices or cupboards usually left open start getting locked. The meeting patterns of executives change and increase in frequency and duration. Managers take away-days together but nothing tangible results. The personnel manager spends more time with the accountant than usual. Even within the personnel department there is greater interest in the contractual details of groups of employees.

Senior management cannot change the habits of a working lifetime and expect employees not to start guessing, and guessing correctly. It would be foolish to go to the employees and say, 'We are having some difficulties currently, and one of the options we are considering is releasing a significant proportion of staff.' It would be foolish because it is only an option, who would be affected is not known, when it would occur is undecided, etc. In these matters it is important for management to be in control, yet so often from their behaviour it is obvious what is being planned. Statements begin to be qualified by phrases such as 'at this moment in time' or 'we have no firm plans as yet'. All are signs of an impending reorganization.

Irrespective of how good employee relations have been in the past, it would be naive of management to imagine that such a state of affairs will continue once redundancies have been announced. Employees will do all they can to protect themselves and their jobs. Research in the United States suggests that the most likely time for a firm to become unionized is when job security is threatened. This is one of the reasons why large non-union companies, from IBM to Marks & Spencer, build job security into their HR creed. Trade union activity is bound to be high when members' jobs are at stake. From a union's point of view far more is at risk in a closure. Its strength derives from its membership, and an unemployed membership is not likely to be able to further the aspirations of organized labour. Additionally, not many unemployed people continue paying their union dues; instead they allow their membership to lapse. (Although many unions make special provisions for their unemployed members.) With these pressures, then, a wise management as part of its planning would do well to work through a doomsday scenario and ask: what if our employees turn against us? What is the worst they could do, and what would be our best response?

Some examples? A specialist production company which was transferring part of its computer operations explored, as a contingency measure, the use of a bureau. It had to. If the release had gone badly the whole computer system could have gone down. A national retailer changing its distribution from small to super-warehouses trained a flying squad of warehouse people and had a contract distribution firm standing by. It had to. If the news of the close-down had gone badly its premier store would have closed, costing millions in lost sales and much unwelcome national publicity. A small pharmaceutical company built up a significant buffer stock of its key products. It had to. If the transfer of the production facility had been handled ineptly product sales and possibly lives could have been lost.

The reasons why such moves should have been taken stretch way beyond the obvious. Firstly, for the team of managers themselves, it is not a normal part of their duties to go through the awful task of laying people off. Managers have not usually had to do so before and consequently are going up their own learning curve. If all the contingencies have been worked through properly they can approach the task in hand knowing that they have control over the situation. That instils self-confidence, which ensures that during the critical first five working days after the announcement the initiative remains with management.

Management will pay dearly if this aspect of contingency planning is ignored. Caterpillar's experience at Uddingston has already been mentioned. For the whole of its time in Scotland since 1956 the firm had enjoyed excellent relations with its unions and the work force. Not enough work was done in contingency planning, and within a week of the closure announcement there was a sit-in which was to last 103 days. Contingency planning also applies to very simple things. For example, if the company fax machine is in the middle of the accounts department it is more likely that confidential faxes will find their way to the work force and the media, sometimes before the appropriate management has even had sight of them. A well thought-out contingency plan can go a long way to prevent the more obvious difficulties.

There is another reason why contingency plans are important, and that is the reaction of the organization's clients and customers. Any reorganization or downsizing is bound to make clients anxious about continuity of supplies or services. It is not unknown for clients to double or triple their orders just to ensure that they are serviced whilst they can seek alternative sources. Organizations with contingency stocks can meet such anxieties with ease. Nor is it unknown for a firm to announce redundancies and then put back the release date because of the influx of panic orders. As can be imagined, the co-operation of employees in such an event will not be at its highest. Management for its part will be wrestling with the twin dragons of overproduction and downsizing.

In preparing for negotiations a wise management will have gone through as many of the 'what if?' scenarios as possible, because once you sit down at the table to negotiate it is difficult in the heat of the moment to be creative and sensible.

Public communications

There needs to be a carefully constructed communications plan covering four major areas:

- The media.
- Clients.
- Suppliers.
- The bank or finance house.

Because of the danger of leaks, it is not advisable to let any of them know beforehand. Each has loyalties which are served by pursuing their own interests rather than yours. When the financial services sector was going through a difficult patch many employees learnt of their dismissal through the media or from clients earlier than through their own management, who were unable to deny the rumours. Many managements were forced to bring release dates forward and make rushed decisions. Once the news is out it is impossible for management to regain the initiative, and any goodwill they may have earned through the way they have handled matters so far will be lost. The rule of thumb is: let your employees know first, and then other interested parties as quickly as possible.

This has implications not just for those who are losing their jobs but for those who remain. If people are released badly the effect of the 'survivor syndrome' (see page 132) is likely to be even more significant.

Press release

The old press adage, 'Bad news is good news', must be anticipated even if for no other reason than that it is probably through the media that your clients will hear of the reorganization. Understandably, success in the media comes from being first with the news. There is more credit to be gained from breaking the story than from working to a timetable constructed by the company. This is particularly true of local radio, which is desperate for local news on an hourly basis.

The best approach is to have a press release ready for local and national media which can be used if necessary. Large downsizings are becoming more common, and hence less newsworthy, so it is unlikely that the nationals will be interested. And, with today's news becoming tomorrow's history, if your announcement comes on the same day as a big news story the events at your organization are unlikely to be of much interest, in which case the press release becomes redundant. A well written press release is likely to be reproduced as it stands because it saves the journalist work. In that case the bad news of job losses can be set in a favourable context of efficiencies and rationalization. If outplacement is being arranged for employees that too can be mentioned.

During the closure of one of the Duracell plants at Crawley a Brighton-based paper picked up the story and ran a feature on the theme of 'The firm that cares', about the job shop the company had set up and featuring the outplacement training which was being given. Three months later there was a follow-up on the number of people who had secured new positions.

All this only went to underwrite Duracell's reputation as a progressive and caring employer.

A senior manager can offer to be interviewed on local radio if the station decides to pursue the story. It is not helpful if the company refuses to comment, because the radio car will easily find a disgruntled employee or two outside the gate at closing time to say a few words guaranteed not to promote the organization in the way it could wish. The general manager of the Glengetti tea company in Leighton Buzzard managed an interview on local radio particularly well, going a long way to maintain a positive image among suppliers and customers as well as preserving the company's reputation in future recruitment. Later a press report announced that the 'immediate release gave the work force the opportunity to take up new jobs as soon as they found them' – a phrase lifted direct from the press release.

Clients and suppliers

The downsizing may be for a good and healthy business reason such as moving to better and bigger premises but good news is often overlooked in the media. Consideration needs to be given to how clients and suppliers can be told of the reasons behind the changes.

Clients respond in one of two ways, either increasing their orders in case the company is forced to allocate goods on a proportional basis or, more commonly, quickly researching alternative suppliers. If used wisely the news of reorganization can be transformed into a selling opportunity.

Suppliers naturally become anxious at the level of credit the organization enjoys, particularly if the manpower reduction is seen as a cost-cutting exercise. Reductions in the labour force could be interpreted as having implications for the organization's credit status. Thus it is wise to think through whether or not plans need to be drawn up to address these issues.

Banks and finance houses

Financial stakeholders also need to be advised of the moves for the same reason as creditors. Their response is usually posi-

positive, since reductions in head count immediately improve financial ratios such as revenue per employee.

Other people

It is worthwhile instructing the switchboard to refer calls about the downsizing to a nominated executive who can quote from the press statement. The local press will often treat the telephonist, who is usually well informed about the organization's activities, as the company spokesperson. On one occasion a line in the local newspaper ran, 'A spokesperson said, "No one really knows what is happening but there are a lot of people crying".' If the closure was only a partial one such a statement would ruin any local reputation as a good employer the firm had built up.

Sometimes people do silly things out of spite when their jobs are taken away. For forty-eight hours after the redundancy announcement, and over the first weekend, it is worth increasing the security patrols at the premises where those affected work.

Chapter 3

Doing it better: operational aspects of outplacement

Preparation

Most organizations have experience of growth, but few have any in downsizing, and consequently it is important to get advice and guidance as quickly and as early as possible. Because outplacement consultancies deal with downsizing on a continuous basis they have a wealth of pragmatic experience which can help the client organization avoid the most fundamental errors.

Operational timing has already been mentioned. As far as the individual people are concerned the main thing is that they should be given assistance *as soon as possible* after they have been told their employment must come to an end. Otherwise the natural responses to job loss – anger, fantasy and depression – prevent them from participating fully in the outplacement process. Yet it is this process which is vital in assisting them to work through these problems. Thus when an executive is being released it is best to have the outplacement counsellor on stand-by, ready to see the person concerned immediately after he or she is given the bad news. Similarly, with large groups of employees it is useful to have consultants immediately available to explain the job search training programmes, job shops and advice or resource centres.

Outplacement consultants are skilled at dealing with the various states of mind of those recently released, so if the organization is going to use such external assistance it is appropriate to get free guidance from the consultancy as early as possible.

Maintaining confidentiality

During the planning stage it is important to maintain complete confidentiality. It is very easy for senior managers to let something slip inadvertently, leave a file out or have sets of manpower figures or cost reduction estimates available to the inquisitive eye. As suggested before, employees will quickly pick up tell-tale signs or notice subtle changes in management behaviour. To go part of the way to meet such difficulties it is useful to give the project a code name. When meetings are called, memos written, files named or when senior managers talk to each other it is less likely that the project will be accidentally leaked. At one publishing firm on the south coast the downsizing strategy was called the 'New York Project'.

Training managers to release staff

It is almost a contradiction that managers should be trained to release people as well as recruit them, but managing a release interview is fast becoming just as much an essential skill as appraisal or disciplinary interviewing. The release interview is not easy because the manager will want to be as sympathetic as possible and concerned to do what is right for his or her subordinates. On the other hand he or she must ensure that statutory obligations are not neglected or difficult precedents created for the future.

Who should do the releasing? Experience has shown that the best person to do the releasing is the manager to whom the employee directly reports. The exception, of course, is the situation when all employees on a particular site will be losing their jobs. Here, for the same reasons, the announcement should be made by the local senior manager who is known by the work force. In my experience the grey-suited man from corporate HQ arouses more anger and anxiety when announcing the closure than if the news is conveyed by the local executive.

Since redundancy is a form of dismissal another reason why it is appropriate for the line manager to undertake the release interview is that should the employee wish to appeal on the grounds of unfair selection it can be done through the HR or personnel department. This would not be possible if the dismissals came from HR management.

Training in how to release thus becomes most important to the success of the downsizing in human terms, not just as regards meeting commercial objectives and statutory obligations. The following sections suggest ways of handling a general announcement to a large group of people about to lose their jobs, and how to undertake a release interview with an individual.

Making a general announcement of redundancy

Often, because the closure of a plant or office is such a significant event, a senior executive feels constrained to make the announcement. In fact it is much better that employees are given the bad news by someone they know and who knows them. Where the numbers involved are small it can be left to the departmental manager to make the announcement to those affected whilst the departmental deputy informs the rest of the department. Where the numbers are more significant it is better for a senior person such as the plant manager to make the announcement in general terms, leaving the departmental managers to deal with the specifics and individual cases.

An example of a typical announcement is shown at the end of this section because it usefully follows a structure which those affected can understand:

- The difficulties the organization has faced.
- The steps that have been taken to overcome them.
- The alternatives that have been explored.
- The releases that have become inevitable.
- Emphasizing that it is the job, not the individual, that has become redundant.
- What happens next.

This structure provides some possibility of individuals understanding why the downsizing is occurring and provides a psychological context for the events.

In my experience most employees sense when redundancy is likely. However, that does not invalidate the case for a structure along the lines suggested. In reaching the decision to close managers will have been living with the problems constantly for a considerable period of time – closure is never the first option. They need to remember that the work force are coming to it for the first time. They need to be told the whys, wherefores and options. Otherwise, the danger is that management will be blamed for being railroaded into hasty and inappropriate decisions. With a little thought, following the principle, 'If I were an employee, what would I want to know and how would I like to be told?' it is possible to construct a suitable announcement.

When Duracell closed one of its plants the works manager's speech was so well done (following the above structure) that spontaneous clapping occurred at the end of the announcement. This was obviously not because people were pleased with what he had to convey. It was an emotional response to a statement delivered clearly, simply and with integrity. Contrariwise, at a food company in Oxfordshire, despite the consultants' advice, a very senior manager, who was not known to the work force, insisted on making a speech which was rambling, unstructured and platitudinous. There was a near riot the moment he finished.

In such a situation there can be no guarantee that the announcement will be received in the right spirit but it will have a better chance of success if it has a structure and logic that the recipients can comprehend, is delivered in language that can be understood and is presented with honesty and respect. Experience has shown that the bad news is best delivered on a Tuesday or a Wednesday. This gives management an opportunity to deal quickly and effectively with the hundred-and-one issues that arise immediately afterwards. Corporate decision-makers usually press local management to make the announcement when it is administratively convenient or when the news will do the least damage in the market-place. Friday is the favoured corporate day but it gives local management little opportunity to retain the initiative and literally *manage* the situation.

Example speech announcing a plant closure

> Friends and colleagues, today I have a very difficult announcement to make.
>
> Before telling you what I have to say, immediately after this meeting I want you to report to your departmental heads or supervisors in your usual place of

work, who will give you further detailed information and answer some of the questions you may have. This is important, because it will not be possible for me to answer any individual questions today. Later in the week there will be opportunities for any personal points or queries to be taken up with me personally.

As you know, the company has been facing exceptional competition from abroad in our XYZ product range. In fact, it is now possible for the competition to sell the XYZ product to our customers for 10 per cent less than we can even produce it for. They can do this because their labour and material costs are significantly cheaper than ours.

Up till now we have been able to stay ahead by investing in better equipment and convincing our major customers of the superiority of our product and its quality. Until now they have listened to us.

Three months ago we were advised by our major customer, who takes over a third of the XYZ product, that next summer we could not expect him to renew his order unless we matched the price of competition from abroad.

Since then the management team have considered whether it is possible to cut costs by further investment in equipment, reducing overheads or using cheaper materials. We also considered the possibility of a significant pay reduction for everyone.

After a great deal of research, thought and review we have decided that we have no option but to cease production of the XYZ product as of June this year. It has not been an easy or quick decision.

The implications are that the life of this particular unit comes to an end because it is no longer viable. To keep the unit going in a loss situation would endanger the future of the whole company.

I want to stress and make it quite clear that no one here is responsible for this situation. No one is to blame themselves or other people here. It is a fact of commercial life.

This means that in *n* months' time this unit will be closed and the jobs will become redundant. Note that it is the job that is redundant, and not any of you as an individual. You have all worked hard and have skills and abilities of which any employer would be proud.

I am personally very sorry to have to be the one to give you this bad news. Each of us will be looking to the next stage in their life and career from now on.

It is not easy at this time when there are so many people unemployed to be releasing people such as yourselves on to the job market. Some will say that the closure announcement should have been made earlier. The reason it was not was that we wanted to explore all the possibilities before taking such a difficult decision. Some would say we should have waited longer, but we wanted you to know as soon as possible.

Each of you will want to know how and when you will be affected. We guarantee to let you have this information as quickly and as accurately as we can. However, we do not have all the information at the moment.

We are still doing our best to work out which departments will be affected. Your managers, who you will be seeing as soon as I have finished, will be giving you details based on what we know at present. These may change but we want to give you the information as soon as possible.

You will also want to know about your entitlements and how much money you will be receiving. Again, you will be given the details later this week.

Those of you who are trade union members, please speak to your stewards and full-time officials. We will be working closely with them throughout this difficult situation. Small comfort, but we have hired the services of professional counsellors who will help you in the process of looking for jobs. They have been very successful in working with people in our situation and that is why we have chosen them.

Finally, may I say thank you for all your support and goodwill in the past. This is not an easy position to find ourselves in or one that we would have wished, but I know I can count on your co-operation during what is going to be a very difficult period for us all.

Thank you for your attention. I ask you now to go

quietly to your work departments, where your managers will have further detailed information.

Planning the release interview

Just as there are ways of selecting individuals for employment, and training is provided in how to conduct a selection or competence interview, so the release interview needs to be handled with equal care. What is said then may be remembered for the rest of the person's life. It also has legal implications if the aggrieved person claims unfair selection for redundancy at an industrial tribunal. Consequently managers involved in this unenviable task should be able to conduct the interview to the highest professional standards. There is no point in hoping that the employee is going to agree with the decision. People will be upset, cross, alarmed, angry; all these things together. What is suggested below is no guarantee or panacea, only some ground rules and principles which for the most part have worked reasonably well, given the inherent difficulty of the circumstances.

Principles

It is the job that is redundant
It is the *job*, not the individual, which is redundant, and at no time should the manager use language which suggests otherwise. The employee is being released, let go, dismissed but *not* made redundant: that happens only to the job. See p. 62 for more on this.

Organizational logic
The logic supporting the redundancy must be organizational, unrelated to the individual or the manager in any personal way. The reasons that are given for the redundancy must be factual rather than subjective. The reasons must be quantifiable and demonstrable not only to the individual concerned but also to the examination of a third party, namely the industrial tribunal. It is a common misconception of line managers that redundancy somehow escaped the unfair dismissal provisions of the employment legislation and that selective

redundancy is open season for subjectivity in managerial selection policy or for settling old scores. Hence the value of having a redundancy policy signed and sealed before the option becomes a reality.

Precedent

Local line managers are notorious for solving today's employee relations problem at the expense of crisis tomorrow. The way the policy is interpreted, the way individuals' jobs are selected and the way the process is handled will all create precedents which will become engraved in the organization's history and culture, and in the expectations of future employees. The question 'Would we choose to act this way next time?' is very valid in this context. In the experience of those involved in this field, an organization facing redundancy for the first time does not usually cut the head count drastically enough and within twelve months has to go through it all over again. Whilst no two redundancy situations are ever the same, the employees affected will expect to receive the same treatment in all respects as those who preceded them.

Personal commitments

Releasing staff who you have known for years is exceptionally difficult. To ease their own anxiety and personal guilt feelings, managers who have to conduct the releasing interview are sometimes led to make promises to their own people that cannot be matched elsewhere in the organization. Inordinate difficulties then occur as other employees demand to know why they cannot expect similar treatment. Common generosities of this sort are an extended period of notice, the use of company facilities, the company car or the extended use of some other benefit or perk. It has to be remembered that those who are released quickly form a network and share information about who is getting what in terms of separation payments and benefits.

Negotiation forum

When jobs are at stake and separation payments are possible, many of the individuals affected, particularly if they are senior, will attempt to negotiate a whole agenda of items, from the use of company facilities to extension of the petrol allowance and all sorts of benefits in between. Think the package through, draw the comparisons and make the package non-negotiable. Some firms have adopted a 'cafeteria' approach where individuals can select their benefits but it has not proved satisfactory. The scheme is difficult to administer once the executive has left, and there tends to be a feeling among those who have been released that others have somehow done better than they.

Final decision

Again, from anxiety and the desperate desire to say something encouraging, managers are tempted to soften the blow with vague hopes of the possibility of job continuation. 'If we win such and such an order . . .' or 'After three months things will be back to normal and I'll give you a call' are not helpful to the individual who is led into waiting for the promise to be fulfilled. Such statements just encourage false hopes which make the eventual job loss that much more difficult to bear.

Platitudinous statements

Finally and obviously the release interview is not the place for platitudinous statements about the linings of clouds or how insignificant the present situation will look in the fullness of time. A moment's thought will reveal how utterly fatuous they are in the circumstances. It is surprising how many people on outplacement programmes will relate how difficult it was for them to restrain themselves whilst their manager was trying to say something positive. In retrospect they were able to appreciate the difficulty of the manager's position, but at the time the trite phrases destroyed any vestiges of management credibility.

Make yourself clear!

It is interesting how different managers can be when breaking the bad news of redundancy to subordinates. Both the following are drawn from real life and both are inappropriate.

Situation 1. The time was a Friday at 5.15 p.m. The manager called in his subordinate, who had been working for the firm for over sixteen years, and said, 'John, as you know, I'm a man of few words. The company's going through a difficult period and I've decided to make you redundant. You need not turn up on Monday and I'll arrange for your money and personal items to be sent on to you. Thanks, John.'

Situation 2. The time was 2.45 p.m. and the subordinate had returned from a good lunch with his managing director. He was met by an anxious personnel director, all ready to outline the separation payments and outplacement provision. The subordinate remarked, 'It was a nice lunch but I didn't understand all he said. He spoke a lot about how the firm is coping with the current difficult situation, but I'm not quite sure what he wants me to do about it.'

Release interview preparation checklist

Before embarking upon a release interview managers might like to work through the following questions.

- How does the person I am seeing meet the criteria of the organization's redundancy selection policy?
- If I am challenged can I give at least three specific and demonstrable work examples of whichever of the following is appropriate?

  Experience.
  Performance.
  Ability.
  Conduct.
  Training or ability to benefit from training.
  Special skills or lack of them.

- If challenged in an industrial tribunal for unfair selection would my reasons and supporting documentation pass the test of third-party scrutiny?
- What do I know of this person's domestic situation? Are there any special issues of which I should be aware, such as:

  Marriage.
  Children.
  Divorce.
  Bereavement.
  House move.
  New mortgage.
  Financial difficulties etc.

- Are there any health matters I should consider concerning this person?
- How has the person I am going to release reacted to difficulty or adverse change previously in his or her career with the company? Is there any indication from the past of how he or she will react to the interview? If so, how can I prepare for it?

How to structure a release interview

Obviously there is no one best way: every situation is going to be both different and difficult. Also, once one person has been told of the redundancy the news will spread quickly and individuals called up will anticipate what is coming. Nevertheless, it is vital for the release interview to be handled well, not only for the individuals directly involved but also to minimize the effects of the 'survivor syndrome' (see page 132). Even if the manager feels that he or she is just going through the motions and the person across the desk knows what is going to happen, it is still better than stories about traders in the City after the crash on 'meltdown Monday' in 1986 hearing their names called out over the tannoy announcing their departure. (The story is apocryphal but tales of people being given black plastic dustbin sacks for their personal belongings and frogmarched out of the trading area by security guards are not.)

The structure that follows is not guaranteed to work, but it will meet most requirements.

Explain the organizational or departmental situation
The reason for doing this is that you the manager will then start in an area which both know about and which is public knowledge. The individual will learn how bad business has been, the difficulties in the market-place, the changes in the technology and all the other reasons why the organization is in difficulty.

Explain the options
An explanation should be given of the action the organization and/or department has taken to rectify the situation. The

options that have been considered can be briefly outlined, with the reasons why they were rejected.

Explain the individual position
State that, after much consideration, the individual job has regrettably become redundant. Say when the job will cease and how long the period of notice will be.

Explain the selection procedure
Refer to the policy document and indicate in broad terms how the individual fits in. This has to be done, because after the immediate shock the first question is 'Why me?' so it is better to make the position clear. It also acts as a quality control stage for the whole process. If the manager cannot fulfil the requirements of justifying the redundancy, then perhaps it should not occur. If the situation cannot be explained in objective and quantifiable terms it is unlikely that it can be justified to the three members of the industrial tribunal, who will be looking for fairness and reasonable actions in all circumstances.

Explain the separation payments
There is no need to go into specific details, just the various components of the package of statutory payments, additional payments, outstanding holiday pay and notice pay arrangements. It is, however, worthwhile mentioning the total separation payment if it has been computed.

Explain what happens next
This is very important. Employees frequently go into a state of shock and really do not know what to do next. Do they go home? See their colleagues? See an outplacement counsellor? Go back to work? Or should they cry?

If for security reasons they cannot go back to the workplace – this frequently happens with data-processing people, sales personnel, traders and the like – it is essential to explain *why* not. It must be made clear that the reason is not that they are not to be trusted, only that it has been known for people in similar circumstances to do considerable harm – crashing the system, giving sales information to competitors, or something similar in the heat of the moment. One firm came up with the reason that 'Our insurers have requested we do this.'

Immediate issues

Ask if there are any immediate issues that need to be addressed. In most cases the individual will be so shocked or confused that questions are not forthcoming, or they are about trivia. An hourly paid employee may ask if he can keep his safety boots. An executive may ask if he or she can fill the car with petrol to get home. This type of reaction is very common and may be due to some form of psychological defence mechanism, the mind hanging on to small things that it can manage. It is not uncommon for the employee to thank the manager for the interview and for his or her time.

This structure has been used satisfactorily for redundancy interviews at all levels. Sometimes employees' individual requirements or questions require the various parts of the interview structure to be reorganized. What is suggested is a curriculum, not a sequential order.

Providing the 'pick-up' or triple interview

When individuals or small groups of employees are being released, the following structure is a proven method of dealing with the situation:

- *First interview* with the individual's line manager following the suggested structure but dealing only minimally with any questions from the employee.
- *Second interview* with the HR representative to cover administrative and separation payment arrangements and dealing minimally with any questions from the employee.
- *Third interview* with the outplacement counsellor, who outlines the services being provided and addresses any immediate issues the individual may be worried about.

This process has several advantages, for the individual(s) and for the organization.

After the shock of the bad news of impending job loss the substance of the interview gets better, with information on financial help and career assistance. It makes the job of the line manager much simpler, and he or she is less likely to get things wrong or make injudicious statements. The contractual and legal entitlements are covered in detail by the HR specialist, who can ensure that everything is correct and meets the statutory requirements.

The final interview, with the outplacement consultant, can be open-ended and may last as long as necessary – certainly until the individual is in a fit emotional state to get home. It is not unknown for the counsellor actually to take the individual home and explain what has happened to the unsuspecting family. On one occasion an individual just wanted to go for a walk to calm down, and asked the counsellor simply to follow him. This the counsellor did for an hour and a half, until the employee was ready to return to the office and talk things through.

All the interviews can be conducted at the place of work but – especially in the case of sales personnel – firms usually hire three rooms in a hotel. In the largest pick-up I have managed I had ten counsellors waiting 'in the wings', two of whom were spare because it was not known how long that part of the process would take.

To ensure that management have maximum opportunity to maintain the initiative and control it is better to hold the release interviews on a Tuesday or Wednesday, preferably in the morning.

Preparing for questions from those released

Almost every time someone is released another question is asked which no one has asked before in a similar situation. In preparing for the release interview managers would do well to anticipate the areas of concern that might be uppermost in the minds of those they are to see. Managers will be expected to answer questions honestly and effectively. Prevarication or 'puff' will not help in what is always a difficult situation. Below are some of the more typical questions that have been asked at release interviews. The list is not meant to be exhaustive, but it covers the main issues and areas of concern for those affected. All have been taken from actual interviews.

For convenience, and also so that they may be used for training purposes, the questions have been divided into 'how', 'what', 'why', 'can I', 'who' and anxiety questions or statements. I have found these categories useful in seminars where managers have been trained in the business of releasing staff. I usually divide the 'releasing group' into sets and ask them how they would respond to a particular category of questions. In a plenary session the group come together and comment on each other's answers.

The subsequent discussion has not only contributed to the individual manager's confidence in undertaking the task but has also thrown up issues of policy. It has also ensured a degree of uniformity of response to those being released.

'How' questions

- How will I tell my wife/husband and family?
- How will I cope with my mortgage?
- How will I get home?
- How can I get a job:
  - At my age?
  - With my qualifications?
  - With no qualifications?
  - With my experience?
  - With my lack of experience?
- How will I manage?
- How do I get my personal things?
- How will you manage without me?
- How much will I get paid?
- How much do I get?
- How will I get a reference?
- How do I appeal against this decision?
- How are you going to tell my colleagues?
- How long can I have my car or other benefits?

'What' questions

- What happens next?
- What will happen to my work/project?
- What sort of reference will I get?
- What is my settlement?
- What happens to you?
- What will you say in my reference?

- What happens to my personal belongings?
- What other parts of the company are affected?
- What do I do now?
- What do you think my chances are?
- What is the appeal procedure?
- What if I refuse to go?

'Why' questions

- Why was *I* chosen?
- Why are you telling me this? (Why not ——?)
- Why are you telling me now? (Why not earlier, why not later?)

'Can I' questions

- Can I say goodbye to my people/friends/subordinates?
- Can I go now?
- Can I have my money now?
- Can I have my reference now?
- Can I keep my car, desk, pictures?
- Can I cry?
- Can I go for a walk?
- Can I think about this?
- Can I smoke?
- Can I telephone my wife/husband? My solicitor?

'Who' questions

- Who will tell my subordinates?
- Who selected me? (Was it you?)
- Who else is going? Who else besides me?
- Who can I tell about this?
- Who will help me?
- Who else knows about this?
- Who will do the job I do? Who will look after my project?
- Who will give me a reference?
- Who can I appeal to?
- Who will have my car, office, desk, etc.?

Anxiety questions/statements

- You've always wanted me out.
- This just goes to show how incompetent you are.
- This is unfair.
- I'm going to take you to a tribunal for unfair selection.
- What if I refuse to go? I refuse to go!
- You're prejudiced against me.
- Well —— you!
- Why didn't you tell me back in ——?
- Just you wait. I'll show you.
- I want to discuss this with my solicitor. I want to see my shop steward/staff representative.
- When is it your turn?
- Who has got it in for me?
- You won't tell my wife/husband/family?
- *You're* all right, aren't you?

Giving notice of redundancy and separation payments

These can be given at the interview, or the person can be passed on to a representative from HR who can go over the details. In either event, it is important for the employee to receive a letter explaining the situation and detailing the dates and timing of the release, because it is unlikely that he or she will remember any of the detail. Whilst not merely fulfilling the legal obligations, the letter should also meet a psychological need in being as jargon-free as possible and written in a caring style. So often this aspect of the release is scripted by company lawyers hired for precision rather than empathy. It should be appreciated that the letter may be kept for a very long while and shown to family and friends. Much more frequently than hitherto it may be produced at an industrial tribunal.

On a separate page or sheet the separation payments should be detailed in a way the individual can understand, compute and check. It goes without saying that the separation pay document should be totally accurate. Counsellors on outplacement programmes are frequently told that the management were so incompetent they could not even get the separation payments right. Errors are understandable, especially when hundreds of people are affected, each with their own unique situation. Accounts staff themselves may be directly affected. Certainly they will be affected indirectly as well as having to contend with the extra strain of confidentiality, so their normal standard of accuracy may be below par. This being so, errors are likely. Consequently a disclaimer on the separation sheet together with an invitation to check the calculations is wise, e.g.:

> Every effort has been made to ensure that these calculations are correct. Please check them very carefully. If you feel there has been an error, or you are not sure how the calculations have been arrived at, or your entitlements are not right, please telephone —— on —— straight away. All queries will be dealt with as quickly as possible.

Giving notice of redundancy to large groups

Sometimes, usually when a total shutdown or mass redundancy is involved, it is necessary to address large groups of people all at once. In such a situation the same structure as the interview can be used. The only exception is that 'What happens next' might actually begin the presentation if junior or local managers are going to tell their people what it means, distribute the redundancy notices and explain the details of separation payments.

Words can hurt: using the word 'redundancy'

It is well established by those interested in the psychology of language that most words have either positive or negative overtones. They are either warm or cold, acceptable or not acceptable, positive or negative. The words 'redundant' and 'redundancy' are very negative indeed and should be avoided wherever possible. It is always the job, position or function that becomes redundant, *never* the individual.

The point is illustrated by an incident at Alcatel when it was decided to pull computing research back to Germany. The plant in Harlow was told that it was redundant and that in three months the facility would be closing. Among those who were told was a young German programmer. Some hours after the announcement she was found in tears. Not having come across the word before, she had looked it up in the dictionary and found it to mean 'useless, of no value'.

One of the major mental blocks for individuals facing the job market is their reduced self-esteem due to being 'redundant'. Getting a new position is initially a process of being turned down by one prospective employer after another, and it is understandable that when people have just had their ego dented the last thing they want is to receive polite turn-downs (PTDs in the jargon).

Employees, then, are forced to leave, released or let go, and this terminology should be used whenever possible, but particularly when dealing with those directly affected. So in letters of notice, a phrase such as 'the job of setter/secretary/budget manager will no longer exist and so, regrettably, we must release you from employment' is much better than 'You have become redundant . . .' It should be remembered that letters giving notice of redundancy are often kept as proof that ex-employees left the job through no fault of their own. Legal exactness should be matched by empathy of style.

Closure and ending: letting people say goodbye

It is now well established in bereavement that it is very important for a grieved individual to 'say goodbye' to the person who has died. When it is not possible the grieving process usually takes much longer. In a not dissimilar way, those who have lost their job need to take their leave of friends and colleagues and to tidy up their workplace. For the manager and some of those who remain it may be less embarrassing to have the redundant person off the premises as soon as possible but that is one of the worst ways to treat an individual who needs to detach him or herself from the job with dignity. Only exceptionally is it necessary to take precautions against malicious intent. One or two instances have been mentioned already but few people are vindictive and only those with access to the central computing facility are in a position to inflict harm or embarrassment.

Where a long notice period has to be served before a closure or there is a large release of people it is not uncommon for a party to be thrown by those affected. At the closure of the Black & White distillery in Stepps, east of Glasgow, a large party was held. Whilst there was no shortage of drink the employees who were losing their jobs were well behaved. A 'raving wake' was held at SmithKline Beecham when several departments were relocated after the merger of the two pharmaceutical giants, again with no ill effects on company property. What is beneficial about such events is that individuals can in some degree participate in and take personal control of the ending of what has after all been a very significant relationship with others at work. Next to the family, most social interaction takes place at work, and thus it matters that it should be 'closed' in the most sympathetic way.

Chapter 4

The individual and outplacement

Understanding the effects of job loss

For those about to take other people's jobs away and for those who are going to work with employees who have been made redundant it is essential to have at least a basic comprehension of what happens to the individual when he or she loses a job. Understanding the issues helps the manager or counsellor to anticipate some of the difficulties the person faces and sets an agenda of items that may need to be addressed. Enforced unemployment has a very significant effect on the individual which can be classified under four main heads.

Personal

Loss of job is directly correlated with loss of self-esteem, and hence the individual whilst unemployed inevitably suffers emotional and physiological setbacks. Being unemployed means being prevented from fitting into society. People without jobs feel they have a negative image and no role to play in society. If Descartes wrote, 'I think, therefore I am,' in industrialized societies the words could be amended to 'I work, therefore I am.' We spend more time at work than in any other activity, not excepting sleep. This vast amount of time therefore constitutes a highly significant component of the way we view ourselves. The work ethic is so deeply ingrained in the cultural psyche that work has taken on a value and a worth in its own right even when the majority do not particularly enjoy what they do.

The problem for the unemployed is one of social reality. When in a job, an individual knows where he or she is in terms of role, functions and expectations, but unemployment takes that certainty away. The individual becomes confused, more so because the future is unclear. Is an unemployed Rolls-

Royce engineer who has just been released an 'unemployed toolmaker' or 'a onetime toolmaker' or an ex-toolmaker or just an unemployed person? Confusion such as this accounts for the behaviour of the recently redundant person who in the early stages continues life as if nothing has happened, going on an expensive holiday perhaps, or taking a break, not doing anything, even refusing to 'sign on': acting as if he or she were not out of work.

The individual also loses friends or encounters changes in social arrangements. The reasons are many. It is thought that people often withdraw from established friendship networks, either because of the perceived stigma attached to unemployment or, more likely, because to participate and not be able to reciprocate is difficult. Being short of money means being unable to pay your way or return a social favour, be it a round of drinks or taking friends' children to the cinema. As Goulder pointed out in 1960, the 'norm of reciprocity' is very strong in shaping individual behaviour.

The framework of time also vanishes for the unemployed. Just as the sailor without a 'dame' in *South Pacific* had no one to put on 'a clean white shirt for', so an unemployed person has no reason to be active. The days become unstructured. It was said that on losing the premiership Margaret Thatcher felt so lost without a very tight timetable that she even became confused about what day it was. With a breakdown of structure comes lassitude, and this can result in lowering of physical and psychological tone. Sleep too is a form of escapism. An unemployed journalist, post-Wapping, called it the luxury of 'daily duvet ducking'. Being asleep gave him the relief of not having to face the fact of joblessness.

Finally, there is the loss of direction. This is particularly acute for managers and executives, who are accustomed to see the life ahead of them as a career with the prospect of successive promotions. Life has both meaning and purpose through working towards career goals and opportunities. With job loss this comes to an abrupt end. The future has no direction because what it holds is not known.

Domestic

Unexpected unemployment brings about a significant breakdown in the major points of the individual's life disrupting both social and family relationships. It can cause a loss of

- active occupational role
- friendship pattern at work
- status
- pride
- the exercise of skill and experience
- professional, trade or trade union membership.

When the pillars of stability are shaken, expectations are removed and relationships are no longer predictable. You are not sure of your status – indeed, if you have status any more. Even how to behave is unclear. What do you say, for instance, when you meet someone new? How do you explain who you *are* without being clear about what you *do*?

As regards marriage, the consensus of evidence is that unemployment increases tensions between husband and wife, and tensions such as this may bring to breaking-point relationships which were already fragile. In other instances, marriage and family life gained a greater sense of closeness through the very difficulties of unemployment. Particularly distressing is the change people see in their relations with their children – a feeling of failure, loss of status, of letting them down, with a loss of affection, even guilt over not being able to provide pocket money. Stories of executives who start to manage the home as they did their subordinates are too legion not to have substance. As one wife put it, 'I married him for better or worse, but not for lunch!'

Financial

The financial effects are more obvious. Reactions to financial loss are as many and varied as there are individuals, but two major responses have been noted. The first, and by far the most common, is to go easy on the expenditure and cut back wherever possible, even when the separation settlement has been generous. Outplacement consultants frequently tell of executives – both male and female – who need much persuading to invest in a more acceptable business wardrobe so that they can present themselves as successful and 'fashionable', even when they have a settlement running in excess of £100,000.

At the other extreme, individuals spend everything. Some because it is a way of pretending that they still have jobs (employed people spend money); some because to have more than £*x*,000 means that you do not qualify for government support. Reputedly several individuals at Uddingston upon the closure of Caterpillar took holidays in the West Indies and bought a wonderful array of consumer goods just so as to qualify for certain benefits. This phenomenon is examined more closely later, in considering the denial phase of job loss.

Resources

The matter of resources particularly affects white-collar and executive employees who in their work situation have access to word processing, paper, telephone, fax and secretarial assistance. Executives tend to find it difficult to present themselves on paper without the usual support systems. The more senior you are the more likely it is that people do things for you, including writing letters on your behalf. Directors sometimes agonize over what to put in a covering letter, and it is surprising how many dyslexics have got to very senior positions. With loss of job comes the loss of 'infrastructure', the support and communication systems which are essential in the search for the next position.

Making the job loss transition

Individuals immediately focus on these practical issues but it is not these alone that need to be resolved. The emotional carousel of feelings that confuse and debilitate the individual, especially during the early stage of job loss, also needs to be controlled. Reaction to job loss is individual, and not everyone responds in exactly the same way. Similarly, some individuals get over the trauma in weeks whilst others never quite recover.

The process is known at the 'job loss curve', an amalgam of the work of many authorities including Hopson and Adams (1976). As has been observed earlier, when someone loses a job the experience is closely akin to bereavement. In fact,

Parkes's book on bereavement (1972) is one of the best orientations to job loss that can be found. On the face of it, it may seem difficult to bracket job loss with the loss of a loved one. Workaholics love their work but by no means is it the same as love within a human relationship, yet the feelings accompanying job loss and the sequence in which they evolve are not dissimilar. The classic job loss model with its six stages is shown in fig. 1. The vertical axis represents the degree of emotionality or activity. It can also stand for personal esteem or ego. The horizontal axis is a measurement of time.

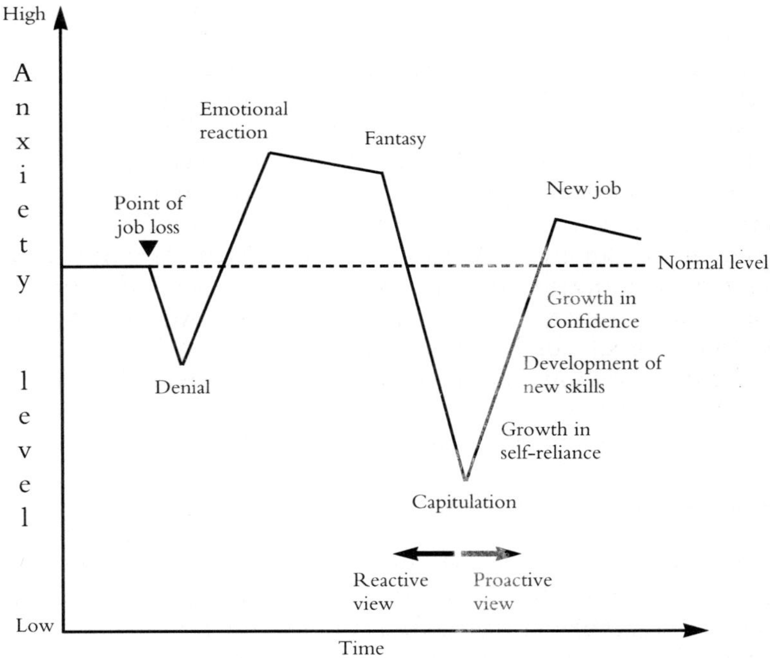

Figure 1. The job loss curve (after Hopson and Adams, 1976)

Denial

The first reaction to job loss is denial or immobilization. The individual refuses to accept the situation. They just cannot fit the news into their understanding of reality. Job loss is something which occurs to other people, not to oneself. The news seems like a bad dream or some form of awful joke – anything but what it really is. Its rejection is equivalent to the mother told that her child has been run over telling the policeman that he must mean another child. People say, and mean, 'I don't believe it.' Sometimes – especially when there is a long period of notice, running into months – they continue to behave as if nothing had happened, with everything going on as before.

Sometimes this form of denial is accompanied by what is called minimization. Many people take a holiday on being made redundant. One explanation is, of course, that it is an opportune time but a more appropriate reason is that a holiday is something that employed people take. Much outplacement counselling time is spent persuading individuals to take a holiday *after* they have secured a new position, and many of the exhortations go in vain.

Many people delay that most public proclamation of personal unemployment, 'signing on'. Signing on at the social security office forces a person to admit to the world and to themselves that they are out of work and for some it is too humiliating a thing to do. Even in severe financial difficulty, some people cannot bring themselves to do it. Another aspect of denial is that outplacement counsellors frequently find that their clients take an inordinate time to get down to constructing their CV. It is as if the CV is painful confirmation of loss of status and security and having to compete in the job market.

Some individuals go on a spending spree, 'retail therapy' as it is sometimes called. Whilst this might be considered strange if not irresponsible, purchasing power is another way of saying to the world, 'I'm still employed really, because this is what employed people do,' or 'My unemployment is so insignificant I can afford to spend this money.'

Anger

Intense emotional activity is the next stage, usually expressed as anger. The individual feels intense emotion about the injustice of the situation. 'It's not right', 'It's not fair,' are common expressions. Anger is a normal element in grief. Individuals actively seek representation of their cause, whether through shop stewards and industrial tribunals at one end of the scale or through solicitors and the High Court at the other. They may fantasize about the collapse of the firm or wish retribution upon those they see as the cause of their situation. In an extreme form, if they are still at work, such feelings may be manifested in physical abuse of machines or products. Odd things may be added to products. On one occasion in my experience the managers' cars suffered slashed tyres and some forthright slogans painted on the bodywork.

Sometimes it is almost as if the individual enjoys the anger, reminding one of the old phrase 'She nursed her wrath to keep it warm.' Frequently anger emerges in the form of general irritability and bitterness. Or it may lead to frenetic activity, with individuals sending off CVs to all and sundry and applying for any job regardless of whether they meet the criteria or not.

During this period, family life is under great strain. The individual may use the members of the family as surrogates on which to vent feelings of bitterness. Spouses frequently complain that their partners almost look for things to complain about, anything seeming to justify an outburst of temper. Job loss strikes at the foundations of self-confidence and personal security. To be angry and blame someone or something else is more acceptable than punishing oneself for 'staying with the firm' or 'choosing to relocate'.

Although it is not true, people may feel that in a real sense they themselves are responsible for the loss of their job, and their anger at themselves is transferred to others as a way of venting their emotion. It is easier to express anger at a specific manager or group HQ or the personnel officer than to recognize that one is just a statistic in changing technology or a marketing decision. Frequently members of the personnel department who used to enjoy good relations with the employees concerned are stunned by the degree of anger that is levelled against them. In a way it is healthy in that the individual chooses to rage at the imagined cause of the pain rather than capitulate to helplessness.

Outplacement consultants are employed so that this anger and high emotion can be purged and vented. Counsellors are often vilified as 'living off the redundant' and taking advantage of the misfortunes of others. Consultants realize that accusations like this are an important part of the purging of grief. If it does not erupt here it will emerge later – on some unsuitable occasion such as an interview where the recruiter is regaled with an account of how the candidate gave the best years of his life only to be rewarded with redundancy.

Fantasy

Eventually the anger burns itself away and in many cases the individual moves on to a stage of fantasy. It takes many and varied forms. Sometimes individuals are so convinced they are irreplaceable that they do nothing about finding another job, confident that before long the phone will ring and they will be invited back to their old job. Sometimes individuals are convinced that their managers have got it wrong, that soon someone from headquarters or a director from the United States will call and reverse the decision. An instance occurred in Sunderland when one of the shipyards was closed. Several managers delayed their job-hunting for months because they felt sure the government would step in with some last-minute funding deal. In one plant where I worked I was having great difficulty motivating a group who were convinced there was going to be a management buy-out. Even when I asked them to look out of the window and see the equipment being loaded on to lorries they were not convinced.

Some fantasize about running their own business but in fact do nothing to begin developing a product or service. Some throw themselves into a frenzy of DIY, redecorating, gardening or patio building, thus maintaining the image of themselves as a 'worker' with much to do.

The fantasy world is so strong a defence mechanism that it is essential for employers not to hint at the possibility of being rehired. In the embarrassment of the moment it is too easy to say, and even mean, something like 'Should the situation change we will, of course, take you back,' or 'If things get better we will rehire.' Statements such as these become lodged in the mind and people hope against hope for reinstatement. They are only too capable of convincing themselves that the job will reappear and there will be a recall. On one occasion the clerical unit of a US-owned firm had been told – mainly to soften the blow – that the US headquarters *could* reverse the redundancies. The staff were ensuring all the files were in the right order for data and alpha-numeric retrieval purposes. When asked why the paperwork was not just being put into boxes as it was, they replied that they were waiting for word that the closure had been rescinded. This despite the fact that their beautifully filed boxes were being taken daily from the office for shredding.

This 'fantasy effect' or 'avoidance behaviour' was noted by researchers in the United States (Sheppard and Belitsky 1966) who found that of 309 male blue-collar workers sixty-nine did not even look for work at all, so confident were they of being rehired by the company. Their partners reported that they just stayed at home. The researchers concluded, not unreasonably, that expectations of recall greatly affect job search behaviour.

The lesson for management is obvious. Ruthless and hard as it may seem, and even if there *is* a possibility of redeployment at a subsequent date, no hint of it should be forthcoming; otherwise it will be seized upon to the detriment of effective action.

Capitulation

When the reality dawns that the job has gone, there is no chance of re-employment, and there are no offers of employment from elsewhere, there comes a feeling of acute despair and apathy. The pain of immediate grief subsides into an abyss of nothingness. People suffer from enormous self-doubt, and whatever they have is not good enough. They consider themselves too old or young, too qualified or not qualified enough, inexperienced or too experienced, too senior or too junior. It is an exceptionally frustrating time when the ego takes most of the knocks. The ever-increasing flow of rejection letters or, what is worse, investing a lot of time in a long application form, and not receiving even the courtesy of a reply, makes matters worse.

Unemployment is essentially a lonely business compared to the team orientation and activity of work. The individual at home has no one to share their plight with or express their anxieties to. If concern is expressed the spouse may worry further, so the inner anxieties are bottled up. The days become blurred, and one day becomes very much like another, increasing the sense of disorientation.

This is one of the most dangerous times because it is when the temptation to give up is strongest. If the person believes that he is of no worth, and is unemployable, the logic of self-promotion in the job market breaks down. 'Why should I do this if I'm unemployable?' 'Why apply only to be turned down or ignored?' Job search seems not just fruitless but a waste of time. Some individuals just close down all activity and become permanently unemployed. This is called being 'broken', and we return to this concept when looking at the stages of unemployment. During this phase the individual's status within the family may change from breadwinner to burden. Husbands, wives and children are not always as sympathetic once the initial shock has passed.

Depression

There is a real danger that individuals become so low that they suffer from clinical depression, believing themselves hopeless: nothing can be done to help them, nor are they capable of helping themselves. It is as if people who have come to think of themselves as unemployable begin to sustain that role actively even when there is evidence to the contrary. Not infrequently it happens that when they are asked to an interview the opportunity is lost because they oversleep or cannot be bothered because they 'wouldn't get the job anyway'. There is a name for this condition: avoidance motivation. Sometimes it manifests itself in odd or unreasonable behaviour, such as not dressing suitably for an interview, turning up late or paying insufficient attention to personal hygiene, all of which militate against being considered seriously for the position.

So it is that in these sorry cases individuals move into what is sometimes called learned helplessness, an unemployment limbo from which many find it impossible to escape. They adapt to the situation, accepting their new world with fatalism. Withdrawal from the world is another fairly common coping mechanism: a refusal to participate, where the individual appears unco-operative and morose. It seems as if they are deliberately shutting out the world as a means of self-defence. A psychological defence is founded on the concept that everyone has a set limit to the degree of anxiety or stress that can be endured. When this level is reached individuals defend themselves emotionally by mental withdrawal from anything associated with the source of the anxiety. The impact of being made redundant and the implications are overwhelming, and consequently the individual decides to block them out. In Neuro-linguistic Programming (NLP) terms this is close to 'chunking down', reducing the information flow concerning reality into chunks small enough for the individual to feel comfortable with them at any one time. It is as if he or she selects which aspects of life to deal with and ignores those which are painful or difficult.

When the whole world has caved in, such defence mechanisms are a natural and healthy way of coping.

Readjustment

Within the individual, eventually, signs can be perceived of a changed coping strategy. The individual has a more realistic understanding of his own behaviour, sees himself not just in terms of his actions but as able in some way to control them. Negative feelings and anger are now more easily resolved. This is balanced by more positive feelings about oneself as a capable human being with intrinsic value, irrespective of the unemployed condition or label. These feelings and thoughts are translated into changes in observable behaviour as the individual begins to identify new possibilities and devote personal effort to their achievement.

Emotional and rational readjustment can have three very different outcomes. The individual can adapt to the new status and join the ranks of the long-term unemployed. The difference now is that he or she no longer regrets having no job and the diminished status that involves. The pleasure of being able to structure the day as one wishes, be beholden to no one and enjoy the aspects of life which are free or at least inexpensive becomes a new and cherished form of existence.

The second outcome would be a complete change of career and job content. The brigadier who was forced to resign because his term was up and there were no chances of a promotion becomes a college bursar, the engine fitter becomes a bouncer at a gaming club, the toolmaker becomes an airport baggage handler. As can be appreciated, such a drastic change requires a radical reappraisal of self, situation and skills. The results can be satisfying. At SmithKline Beecham, for instance, a maintenance supervisor with a keen interest in gardening joined a small firm of landscape gardeners.

But by far the most usual outcome is that the individual re-enters the job market in the capacity he or she held before, employing the same skills and experience. The job title and even the industry may be different but the job is essentially the same: the shipbuilder from the North East joins a firm on the south coast building pleasure craft, the toolmaker from Watford makes model brass cannons for the gift market. Frequently, executives gain a promotion on re-entering work, becoming directors of smaller firms rather than heading a department in a large organization.

So it is that in the job search people discover new things about themselves. Through the discovery they develop new skills and become aware of dormant abilities. In effect the process is one of growth and personal empowerment. No one would wish to go through the process again, nor would they wish it on others. But in retrospect people will not infrequently say that from losing their job and what they had to do to recover they are far more confident in themselves as individuals.

The stages of unemployment

What happens to the unemployed needs to be understood for two reasons. It assists in understanding the context of outplacement. More important, it shows how vital it is to provide support as quickly as possible for those who are released, especially for hourly paid and junior employees.

Work on the stages of unemployment began during the slump of the 1930s and the major findings, though added to, have not changed. Essentially, it is understood by bringing together the psychological and economic factors associated with unemployment. The notion is that the unemployed move through several distinct and recognizable stages which constitute a sequence from optimism to pessimism to fatalism.

Initially there is a confidence in one's ability to find work. One still has skills and the reputation of a good employee. Getting work is just a matter of contacting agencies or responding to adverts, neither of which is seen as taxing. During this stage there is still the separation and/or redundancy money, so financially nothing changes drastically. People continue their usual level of expenditure. Some will take a holiday – 'they deserve it' – or buy some consumer durable 'now they can afford it'. Whilst there is cash there is confidence. Optimism is the characteristic of this stage.

Slowly it becomes apparent that getting a job is not going to be as easy as was thought, and cash becomes tight. Anxiety and stress begin to rise. This is the stage of pessimism, a period when self-doubt abounds. In the final stage the money runs out, as do savings, and there is a real deterioration in clothes and belongings which it is not possible to replace. Individuals become convinced, not that there are no longer any jobs out there, but that they are unemployable. Hope turns to hopelessness and all efforts at self-help cease. The individual is apathetic and broken.

The social scientist Jahoda (1979) put it this way:

> We have distinguished four basic attitudes: the predominant one is resignation, a more active one we named unbroken; and two deteriorated forms we call despair and apathetic. As we look back on these two forms, it now appears that they are probably but two different stages of a process of psychological deterioration that runs parallel to the narrowing of economic resources and the wear and tear on personal belongings.

Thus whilst all those made redundant may start their employment search differently because they are different, if they are not successful all end up in the same final stage of fatalism.

Perhaps it is this area that offers clues to the different success rates of outplacement and government schemes for the long-term unemployed, with the former being far more successful. Outplacement starts immediately, while the government schemes do not. There are other factors, of course: 'better' people will get jobs more quickly, leaving those who are less attractive among the lump of the unemployed. Employers are noted for prejudice against those who have been out of work for an extended period, viewing them as set in their ways and in the culture of unwaged leisure.

The findings suggest that the sooner the outplacement process is begun the better. Some employers have decided, for various reasons, including budgetary ones, not to fund outplacement immediately following the redundancies. Support is reserved for those still unemployed after three months. My experience of such programmes is limited, but in my view it is better to provide whatever services you can afford as quickly as possible, to forestall the sad progression from optimism through pessimism to fatalism.

Counselling: have your outplacement people the skills?

Something needs to be said about counselling, because outplacement is essentially a counselling process. Many personnel people drift into it on the basis that they have the knowledge of CV production and interviewing, perhaps coupled with recent experience of the anguish caused by job loss. Outplacement is more than developing skill in job search and receiving sympathy. What follows is an introduction to some basic elements of counselling so that in selecting an outplacement consultancy the client can form his or her own opinion as to whether he or she is selecting a team of trainers or a team of counsellors. In outplacement it is the latter who do the better work, because the subject is essentially about empowering people and planning strategies of coping and confidence growth.

Forms of assistance

When faced with unemployment an individual places a whole range of demands upon a counsellor. At the basic level it is a question of straightforward help in terms of information about State benefits or the job market, or making telephone calls to local employers to discover job opportunities and arrange interviews.

It may be straightforward teaching on how the job market

works or what questions to expect at interview. Teaching and helping, whilst essential, are not counselling. Counselling is assisting people to take more control of their own lives and destinies. It is essentially about enabling people to recognize their situation and, of their own volition, to do something about it. A healthy functioning individual is one who can recognize the situation, envisage a realistic future and control his or her behaviour until part or all of that future has been achieved.

In outplacement terms this means the individual recognizing that unemployment is not the end of the world, that they have abilities, skills and experience which can make a contribution to society, that they can identify where that may be and so take steps to achieve the goal. It may not be a similar job, but that is not the point. What is important is for the individual to be in control and responsible for his or her own actions and choices. Counselling is a way of assisting.

There are a range of issues where counselling is appropriate. The list in figure 2, page 80, is not exhaustive but touches the main areas. Some attempt has been made at classification but life is not compartmentalized and a change in one area will affect others.

Counselling comes in various forms but the style favoured currently within outplacement is known as client-centred counselling. In the UK this is due largely to the great work in introducing counselling skills to industry of Tony Milne, who was for many years Director of Counselling at CEPEC. Outplacement is client-centred, and for most of the time non-directive, because the responsibility for direction, development and behaviour remains with the individual who is outplaced. The aim of this client-centred counselling is to assist the individual, through his or her abilities, to realize their full potential.

In corporate outplacement it should be remembered that most individuals receive counselling almost against their will, for they would much prefer to be employed and not have to go through the outplacement process. Many are in a high state of anger or anxiety and the outplacement counsellor is frequently the first available target. The released employee will often refrain from showing anger at the firm, because that might jeopardize the possibility of a return or affect an

Personal
- Skills and abilities
- Age
- Lack of qualifications

Health
- Personal fitness
- Weight loss or gain
- Sleeplessness
- Depression/anxiety
- Skin problems

Relationships
- With spouse, children, relations and friends
- Being alone
- Being rejected

Status
- Loss of symbols of achievement, e.g. company car
- Perceived shame at claiming benefits
- Inability to be generous in social situations

Experience
- Insufficient experience at work
- Too much experience at work
- Too many/too few jobs

Job search
- Promoting self
- Being turned down
- Being interviewed
- Not working again
- Getting a job offer
- Choosing a job

Future job
- Doing something different
- Taking a step up/down/across
- Initial lack of job security
- New/different technology or systems
- Working with younger people
- Relocation
- New relationships

Psychological
- Being ashamed
- Being frightened
- Being alone
- Feeling inferior or of no worth
- Feeling insecure
- Feeling anxious or depressed

Figure 2. Counselling curriculum for those with no job.

employment reference. Equally people will try to contain their feelings at home so as to reduce tension in the family. The counsellor is left as the most convenient target.

The features of counselling

Counselling is a process within a relationship, with the counsellor being a catalyst rather than a trainer or mentor. The process involves a whole armoury of skills but the features of the process should be constant. For Carl Rogers (1951 and 1958), the American psychologist, they could be epitomized as empathy, genuineness and warmth.

Empathy

Empathy is best understood as sympathy-plus. For Rogers it is the ability to enter the world of the other person without loss of oneself, thereby achieving full understanding of the other person's situation, feelings and aspirations whilst retaining personal objectivity. To pick up on an earlier analogy, a personnel manager who has been released can show a great deal of sympathy in terms of emotional support, care and concern, but that is not enough. In selecting counsellors for my own consultancy I always ask how they counsel those who have just lost their job. If, during their answer, they dwell on their own redundancy, the effects it had on them and how they find it useful to show people they know 'what it is like because they have been there' I begin to grow alarmed that they may be great on sympathy but weak on empathy. Whilst there is a valid place for self-disclosure, telling someone who has just been released how you got through it yourself is not always the most helpful approach.

In constantly talking about personal experience, however relevant, the counsellor cannot be monitoring the experience, perceptions and world of the person he or she is working with. Empathy means participating in the pain of the other person and not just supporting them. This requires great skill, especially if the time available, for reasons of budget or sheer number of people to be seen, is limited. Any hint that the counsellor is processing the individual and the relationship is flawed.

Genuineness

Working with another person requires trust and honesty.

Particularly in outplacement, where the organization is paying the fees, the released employee could rightly be sceptical about the motivation and first loyalty of the counsellor. Sometimes they are challenged in a jocular fashion: 'You must be the only industry doing well in this recession.' More forcefully, when I was working with a lighting firm, some said, 'You're like undertakers who hang around a hospice – you must hang around firms in trouble, hoping they'll die.'

Outplacement consultancies are, of course, commercial organizations. Nevertheless their counsellors must display a genuineness and sincerity of concern when working with outplaced individuals. Communication between the parties has to be open and honest all the time. I seem to remember my response to the undertaker challenge was something along the lines of 'If you swap the terms to "ambulance driver" and "hospital" I agree with you. We're being paid for this service, but we only won the contract because we were successful elsewhere. We are a successful consultancy because we do care about the people we work with.' It is only by being honest in the relationship that the counsellor earns the right to challenge the honesty of thought and action of the individual who is being assisted.

Warmth

This is Rogers's third tenet. 'Unconditional positive regard' is the jargon term but 'warmth' describes it very well. The individual needs to know that you accept them for what they are irrespective of their background or condition. People who have just lost their job are sensitive about their age, their experience, their lack of qualifications and their interpersonal inadequacy. In expressing real warmth the counsellor can rekindle in the individual a feeling of self-worth.

Warmth is not so much a skill as an attitude. Any counsellor who is concerned about status or background, or who likes to select the type of person they work with, is unlikely to have this gift of unconditional positive regard. Warmth in the relationship is like warmth in spring, necessary for growth.

Other aspects

Other skills include those suggested by Robert Clarkhuff (1974), namely confrontation, concreteness and immediacy.

Confrontation is necessary because the individual needs to be assisted into reality. As we have noted, those released may have unrealistic ideas about their abilities or career expectations. This can apply to both the executive and the hourly paid. Fantasy is important; it is good for people to have a dream, but, like business targets, it must be within the realms of reality. In my time I have worked with a fitter who at the age of forty wanted to become a brain surgeon and a research director aged fifty-five who aspired to become general manager of a large manufacturing firm. Both were being unrealistic. Take an attractive, well-spoken female bottling assistant with excellent interpersonal skills who wants to be an air hostess and you move into the realm of the possible, as in the case of one young woman on a contract I managed. Or a stores assistant who wants to work in a bank, or a computer specialist in UNIX who wants to become a consultant – these are not unrealistic. But reality is revealed through skills of confrontation, helping the individual to recognize – and be content with – the differences between the real person and the ideal self.

Confrontation in a supportive way is a sign of a good counsellor. The individual is challenged but still valued as someone of worth who has much to offer. There is an additional imperative here. Because so many managers are inept at interviewing, and good outplacement is excellent at coaching individuals to be brilliant at interviewing, it would not be difficult to get people through interviews for jobs they would only fail at once they started work. Confrontation goes some way to shaping realistic career aspirations in the mind of the participant.

Many people have difficulty understanding their feelings as they go through the job transition process and it is here that *concreteness* is helpful. What does the person really mean when he says he feels 'pissed off with himself for allowing the redundancy to happen' or when she says she feels 'so gutted she can't face another interview'. During the pain of the outplacement much of the language is kinaesthetic. That is to say, it is about feelings rather than what can be seen or heard. For example, people feel . . . down, walked over, kicked, thrown, broken, flat, shocked, frozen, etc. Counsellors should know what such terms mean to the individual concerned. Anxiety, pain and frustration can be expressed in many ways and counsellors need to know the nuances of the individual's language to work with him or her effectively.

Interestingly, the individual begins to move forward and integrate the pain of redundancy positively when the kinaesthetic language gives way to more visual phrases. Individuals develop a vision, begin to see ahead, form a clearer picture of their position and look forward more. (Readers interested in language changes during the counselling period should read up on NLP techniques or take a course in this valuable skills-based area.)

Finally, *immediacy* continues to keep the person in the here-and-now. For much of the transition process individuals look back to the halcyon days of job, salary and friends. Those who have been made redundant before look ahead with fear and dismay to the endless round of sending off speculative CVs and continually filling in application forms. Keeping the person in the present aids activity in the job search process.

Dwelling in the past or the future can actually inhibit doing anything positive about the present. The individual needs to be encouraged whenever possible to operate in the present. Val Lowman, a management advisor in Twickenham, continually asks the people she works with, 'How are you feeling right now?' 'Where are you right now?' 'What are you going to do right now?' She gets remarkable disclosures from the people with whom she is working. Sharing feelings and stimulating the ability to express them is not only cathartic but in outplacement assists the individual in developing the rapport and interpersonal skills that are so vital to being able to present well at interview.

The role of the outplacement counsellor

What does the counsellor do? Each case is, of course, different but the following gives an indication of what one would expect of a professional in this area. Again, it comes in the form of a sequence which is typical rather than absolute but he or she should be able to talk through each of the stages from both knowledge and experience.

The recognition of job loss

The trauma of job loss, as we have seen from the job loss curve, brings about a perceived unreality – that the unacceptable has not really occurred. The person *must* recognize the job loss; otherwise no further work can be accomplished. In crude terms, it is the task of the counsellor to pull the ostrich's head out of the sand; to keep the focus on reality.

Questions can usefully promote discussion about the job loss and make denial difficult. So, for example, questions such as:

Who told you the bad news?
What was said?
What did the letter say?
Who knows about this?
Who have you told?
Who are you going to tell?
When are you going to apply for benefit?

almost force the individual to go through the job loss experience again. It is exceptionally painful for the counselled and for the counsellor but it helps the reality of the situation to dawn so that the process of reconstruction can begin.

The venting of feelings

Job loss brings about a whole Pandora's box of feelings ranging from anger, sadness and guilt through to helplessness. Some of the emotions have been discussed earlier. I mention sadness here because frequently the individual just cries. Tears are beneficial and cathartic in themselves but the reasons for the sadness need to be identified and worked through with the individual. Again, questions are helpful:

- What are you sad about most?
- Who do you miss?
- What do you regret?

After a while the skilled questioner can bring about a subtle change with:

- Will you miss everybody?
- Could there be some things you are relieved about?
- What will you miss least?

HR people are sometimes taken by surprise when guilt is expressed but frequently individuals feel as if they were in some part responsible for their job loss. Expressions such as 'If only I had worked harder' or 'I knew I was not getting on with people but did not do anything about it' are often heard. Again the individual needs to be coaxed, preferably non-directively, into the reality of the situation, that it is the job that has gone and not necessarily as a result of their performance within it.

Doing without the job

This is difficult. Essentially the counsellor wants the individual to make a full time job of getting a new one, but frequently, especially when individuals work their notice, they spend far too much time completing projects which are of very little significance for the releasing firm. Individuals have to learn that their main priority is to look after themselves and their own prospects rather than that of the firm. HR directors in closedown situations where they themselves will be job seekers are most prone to this. Whilst ensuring everyone else is cared for, they ignore their own needs.

Delaying decisions

Some individuals start firing from the hip. They send out CVs like confetti and tell the world and its dog that they are ready for the next stage in their career. Some even decide to sell up, or relocate or even get divorced. They burn themselves up in a super nova of activity. Again, a difficult response for the counsellor who obviously wants the individual to work, but in a structured and focused way. Sometimes with this hyperactive response it is almost impossible to get the individual to sit down and in a methodical and logical way to undertake a SWOT analysis or to review their medium to long term objectives.

Help the person through

Counsellors know what the individual is going through and what is being felt. In a non-directive, non-platitudinous way the individual can learn that these acute yet legitimate feelings are 'normal' and healthy. The art of telling what are called 'Friend John stories' is useful here. The counsellor tells the story of a person not too dissimilar to his or her client and what they went through, how they felt and what the outcome was. The individual can then take what is relevant to his or her situation. If the counsellor can 'calibrate' the individual (recognize by non-verbal signs from the individual what is useful and what is not), then that part of the story can be elaborated upon.

Whatever technique or tactic is used, what needs to be achieved here is for the individual to know that what is being felt is a part of the healing process; that the hurt and the confusion is part of recovery. Just as not being able to laugh after an operation because the stitches pull or stiffness after cramp are physical signs that the body is healing itself, so the expression of emotions is a psychological sign of a return to normality.

Watch for games

Some individuals, because of their anxieties, play games in order to defend themselves in the unknown territory of unemployment. A frequent game is 'I do it your way'. Here the individual does *exactly* what he or she is told by the counsellor. On failure, it is, of course, the counsellor's fault. Another is 'It won't work'; for instance, a very shabby letter is sent off quickly to fifty hunters. No replies are gained so the statement is confirmed. 'There are no jobs out there' is also popular because then the individual does not have to look!

Some defence mechanisms are more serious, such as alcoholism, and any dependency which needs to be treated must be looked for and, if the pathology is significant, the individual will need to be referred.

Without claiming to offer a complete overview of counselling skills, there should be enough of substance here to assist in the questioning of prospective outplacement providers. With the employment market in recession many recruitment agencies are adding outplacement as part of their portfolio of services. There is no reason why they should not do so, provided it amounts to more than CV construction and interview practice.

Questions to ask prospective outplacement counsellors

With a clearer idea of what is involved in counselling and the qualities it demands of those who undertake it, the HR manager is better placed to weigh up the calibre of the people an agency can call on. These are the sort of things he or she will want to ask them:

- Tell me about your counselling experience.
- What style of counselling have you found useful in helping people made redundant?
- What qualifies you to counsel someone who has been made redundant?
- What kind of people have you worked with most in your outplacement assignments?
- In outplacement situations, what kind of person do you prefer to work with? Why?
- What do you find difficult about counselling the redundant?
- When would you refer someone you were working with to another counsellor?
- Without breaking confidentiality, give me an example of how you have shown empathy towards someone you have recently counselled.
- What do you think will be the major issues and anxieties of the people you could be working with on this assignment?
- At what stages of the outplacement process is counselling more appropriate?

Differences between men and women

'Are the counselling needs different as between men and women?' is a question frequently raised. Experience suggests that it depends upon the significance of the contribution of the individual's earnings to the household budget. Where the woman is the main breadwinner, or her remuneration is crucial to the family's standard of living, then the job loss is just as traumatic.

However, working with large numbers of women over the last decade or so has suggested some apparent differences. This is an area for proper research but in my experience women adjust to joblessness more quickly than men. Possibly it is because society allows women the role of full-time mother or housewife more readily than it allows men the equivalent roles full-time. In counselling sessions women hardly ever talk about the perceived shame or embarrassment of their unemployed status, whereas this problem is frequently high on the male agenda.

Social networking and how the sexes go about it are another perceived difference. The size of the network – that is, friends, colleagues, people you know or have been in contact with – is about the same for both sexes, around 150 people. But for males most of the network is work-dominated, whereas women's contacts have a much broader social sweep. Women appear to have less difficulty in letting people in their network know that they are unemployed and looking for work. Men seem happier pursuing openings through advertisements and agencies rather than using their network as a source of potential job opportunities.

Outplacement counselling process

As the individual moves through the stages of dismissal to job offer there are usually distinct phases in the counselling process.

The phases are not necessarily discrete and further work may be needed in a particular area after a setback or a disappointment. For instance, failure to achieve a particularly desirable job frequently rekindles all the feelings of anger and bitterness which were experienced at the time of the redundancy. In another situation, continual failure to get a senior position in a desired industry or location may require a reassessment of personal career goals.

Outlined here is the usual sequence of the counselling phases occurring during the outplacement process:

- *Help the person face up to the crisis.* Taking job loss as a fact of working life which others have been through and most will experience during their career. To be able to let go of the previous position and, if necessary, the friendships that went with it.
- *Venting anxiety.* Purging anger and/or anxiety from the individual so that they see themselves and their situation as

an opportunity for personal growth and future success.

- *Objective review.* An honest examination and acceptance of personal skills, talents, abilities and experience which can be profitably employed.
- *Objective vision.* A realistic career goal which matches their desires with their abilities and personal and domestic situation.
- *Motivation and confidence.* Kindling in the individual the desire to enter the job market through personal effort and commitment to success.
- *Honest presentation.* Enabling people to present themselves to prospective employers with honesty and integrity, confidence and maturity.
- *Realistic evaluation.* Examining suitable job offers and only accepting a position which meets the mutual legitimate requirements of the self and the prospective employer.
- *Personal development.* Using the new position to grow and develop new skills and abilities rather than repeat previous successful skills sets.

Psychometrics in outplacement

A host of advantages accrue from the use of psychometrics in career counselling and outplacement. Most of the better consultancies use personality and ability questionnaires as an aid to working with individuals. At its most basic level the use of questionnaires opens up discussions and legitimizes the individual taking himself/herself in a way that is different from his/her specific work context. Discussion of feelings, hopes and anxieties, which is very necessary if the released individual is to work through the transition process of job loss to career move, also becomes possible.

Whilst it is unlikely that the questionnaires or other instruments will tell individuals anything new about themselves, they will provide what are called normative data, that is, data on how they compare with others. Using the 16PF, for instance, the individuals may know that they are assertive and self-sufficient but the indication that they are in the ninetieth percentile for both these traits will be significant for the individual. The counsellor also gains a more accurate picture of the person.

A reality check upon the individual is gained in this way. Sometimes ego defence mechanisms go into overdrive as part of the coping mechanism, sometimes people fantasize about their attributes or interpersonal skills and a completely different picture emerges from the questionnaire, sometimes the reverse happens when individuals underestimate themselves. Either way, the questionnaire provides fecund ground for counsellor and counselled to till and harvest together.

Through discussion of the dispositional profile people will come to know themselves in a more scientific way, and certainly it will provide language and concepts which can be used in response to appropriate interview questions. The profile is useful in senior appointments, which are just as concerned about influencing skills and personal style as about technical or functional abilities. Where individuals understand themselves and their traits and abilities the better their self-presentation will be. In addition, they will be better able to select a position which is compatible with their skills and needs. In senior positions many executives are released because they no longer fit or, more commonly, do not get on with a newly appointed chief executive. Personality data will help the individual select the people he or she can work with best.

What is also interesting for both counsellor and counselled is the career theme information. Most individuals are drawn to a career in what they are good at. Analyticals go into system analysis, extroverts into sales, practicals into production, creatives into PR, but sometimes the questionnaire data suggest an interesting possibility not thought of before. This is not to say that the banker with the profile of a diplomat could or should join the Foreign Office, or that the teacher whose profile is that of a successful salesperson should go into selling. However, if there is a strong desire to do something different now that redundancy has made it possible, this is useful information. Questionnaire data is one more piece in the information jigsaw that an individual assembles in reaching a career decision. Like all decisions, the more quality information available the more apposite the eventual choice.

Since many employers and headhunters use psychometrics as part of the selection process, it is also useful for the individual to have gone through the process already. The assessment is demystified and the anxiety is taken out of the process.

Where the consultancy has a qualified psychologist the psychometric data can give an important insight into the individual's clinical state. Unfortunately some, although fortunately few (in my experience about 0.5 per cent), are so shaken by job loss that they are not in a fit state to begin work on their career change, and any pressure in that direction could make the situation worse. Outplacement consultancies are retained and assessed on the length of time it takes to get people to their next position – a proud statistic quoted by most of the entries in the *Corporate Directory of Career Change and Outplacement*. Not all individuals are up to the encouragement and motivational pressure they will receive from the consultancy and it is pertinent that any possible difficulty is discovered early.

The following example is an excerpt from a dispositional profile for a female executive aged forty-two. It gives a flavour of the use of psychometrics in outplacement.

Excerpts from a dispositional profile for a female executive aged 42 years

Rosemary presents herself as a highly independent extrovert: an outgoing, warm, participative person who actively seeks the company of others. If anything, she is becoming more dominant and assertive than hitherto (perhaps because she has held a more powerful position and she now feels more confident in her abilities and skills).

An interesting aspect of the profile is that Rosemary is far more reflective than one usually finds in extroverts. She spends much time 'inside her head' and this will be of great help to her as she works through the next stage or transition of her career.

The career themes suggested by her profile are as follows (in rank order of importance):

Venturesome – Influential
Creative – Expressive
Analytic – Investigative

Nurturing – Altruistic
Mechanical – Operative

This ranking would suggest that Rosemary would be ill-advised to take up a position in the caring professions (she was actually considering charity work) unless it included a very high content of leadership and power. Her profile suggests that she would make an excellent manager, a reasonable colleague but a poor subordinate. Many of the caring professions have a very high team/committee orientation, which is not Rosemary's preferred management style or environment.

What is interesting in the profile is the high score for the Creative–Expressive career theme. Rosemary is exceptionally bright (I estimate in the top 2 per cent of the general population) but she also has the ability to display divergent as well as convergent intelligence – that is to say, creative as well as logical approaches. I suspect that one of the frustrations of her current and previous positions is that much of her work and the way that it is presented are prescribed by statutory, professional and commercial requirements. It may be that this aspect of Rosemary's disposition has waited long enough and she is allowing it to flower.

The profile suggests that approval and recognition are very important to Rosemary. In career terms, this means that she would be ill-advised to pursue a career as an independent consultant. Rosemary would do well in activities which require her to persuade or influence others or indeed commit others to lines of action.

The Integration and Mental Health scores are positive, and so Rosemary will have no difficulty in coping emotionally with her chosen career transition and the stresses it will bring. Her usual way of working is to set herself specific targets, envisage them and then act. I can see no reason why this approach should not be continued once direction has been identified.

Rosemary's career options

Through the psychometric material repertory grid analysis and interview, it is my view that Rosemary has the following career requirements.

Dispositional requirements

- Opportunity to demonstrate professionalism publicly through quantifiable results.
- Opportunity to grow, learn and develop.
- Opportunity to manage and to gain social approval and recognition.
- Opportunity to take risks and show daring.
- Opportunity to be with and compete with others.

Organizational requirements

- Large enough to have social and status recognition.
- Culture of high standards and values (professionalism).
- Organization in a state of change or flux where precedents are minimal.
- A culture where effecting actual change is possible, recognized and rewarded.
- A culture of management by objectives.
- A culture where considered risk is encouraged.

Job content requirements

- Dealing with absolutes rather than 'soft' areas, e.g. working with money, numbers – giving quantifiable results.
- Project-oriented rather than predictable and repeated flow of work.
- High managerial content.
- High potential for exercising personal influence.

As can be seen from this example, there is much information which the individual can use both in selecting a particular career direction and in talking about themselves during an interview. Such questionnaires provide what is called normative data. Most people going through outplacement are likely to know their personalities quite well. However, what they might not be aware of is how they compare to other people. For example, it might be helpful to know that you rank in the top 5 per cent of managers for qualities such as self-sufficiency or enthusiasm.

For those who are selecting an outplacement consultancy it

is important to ensure that this aspect of the counselling process is being undertaken professionally. Only psychologists who qualify for associate status of the British Psychological Society or for full membership of one of the Society's divisions are qualified to administer the whole range of questionnaires. Some publishers of tests provide training in their usage and competency here should be verified.

To conclude this section on psychometrics there follows some questions it might be helpful to ask of the consultancy's psychologist when selecting an outplacement firm to work with your people:

- How are you qualified to do this work?
- Which questionnaires, tests and instruments do you use with your clients – and why?
- At what stage in the process do you use psychometrics?
- What are the advantages of psychometrics in outplacement?
- What are the difficulties of psychometrics in outplacement?
- Who has access to the results?
- What topics do you concentrate on during the feedback session?
- Do you write up the results for the client?
- What issues arise from your feedback?
- How do you ensure confidentiality?
- Do you collate the information in any way?
- Do you undertake follow-up studies with your clients?
- If necessary, do you ever refer your clients?

Chapter 5

What happens in outplacement (1) executive services

Basically there are three generic types of outplacement service that are available to an organization which is releasing staff, namely:

- Executive one-to-one service.
- Job search training for groups.
- Job shops or advice centres.

When appropriate I have included examples of exercises and illustrations of aspects of outplacement. The object is not that the HR director and his or her team should be able to devise an outplacement programme so much as that they should have a better understanding of what is involved. It is to be remembered that methods for executives and for hourly paid staff are not mutually exclusive.

Unless the purchaser knows something of the process and what is involved it is very difficult to distinguish between one outplacement consultancy and another. Like all consultancy, outplacement is expensive but, unlike other consultancy work, large projects in downsizing or merger occur infrequently so it is important to be able to make the *right* choice on an informed basis. This section sets out in some detail what can be reasonably expected of an outplacement consultancy so that the purchaser can ascertain what is on offer, what is actually being provided and whether or not it is suitable.

Because outplacement generates high fee levels, many consultancies now employ professional sales and marketing personnel to promote their range of services. Decisions about which consultancy should be based on issues concerning content, appositeness and quality, not on the impression created by the directors and the location of the offices. What follows will provide some basis for making an appropriate choice, for monitoring the project and for assessing its quality.

We can start by outlining the corporate outplacement options from which the releasing company will have chosen before going on to see how they are implemented at the level of the released employees.

For executives

- Use an external outplacement consultancy.
- Set up own outplacement facility staffed by external consultancy staff.
- Set up own outplacement facility staffed by own personnel trained by external consultancy.
- Direct counselling without centre facility completed by external outplacement staff.

For staff and manuals

- Provision of an on-site or off-site job shop staffed either by outplacement consultants or by internal personnel.
- Provision of training programmes either by outplacement consultants or by internal staff.

For all employees

- Financial advice by independent advisers.
- Positive retirement programmes for those who qualify.
- 'Start your own business' for those suitably qualified.
- Specialist programmes where appropriate, such as self-presentation and dress.
- Health and fitness.
- Personal computer skills.

Executive services

The released individual enjoys a one-to-one relationship with his or her career counsellor. Fees for the service are around 15 per cent of final salary plus an entry or administration charge of anything up to £6,000. Most of the larger consultancies set a minimum fee of around £4,500. Since the time for getting a job is about the same whether you are earning £100,000 or £35,000, and the costs are similar for servicing either candidate, there is much competition for the top end of the market. Human resource directors should remember that *everything* is negotiable. Consultancies will usually give discounts for exclusivity with released executives over an agreed period. Large contracts for five or more executives can always be negotiated, and several consultancies begin to discount around this figure.

The larger consultancies will provide for the released executive a centre or an office facility from which he or she can work to achieve the next stage in their career. The centre is usually equipped with secretarial and administrative support services for CV and mail shot facilities. As mentioned earlier (p. 28), the better consultancies also provide library services and access to large business databases such as Textline. Most consultancy premises have limited space, and obviously the consultancy would prefer such accommodation as is available to be given over to highly paid executives.

Executives who have been released are usually assigned to a nominated counsellor and have access to an occupational psychologist who undertakes careers advice and specialist counselling where necessary.

In selecting an outplacement consultancy it is of course wise to visit the facilities available for those being counselled. An open-plan office is usually available in which individuals take a desk on a first-come first-served basis. Some days, centres get very crowded so it is useful to ask the ratio of desks to executives. Usually one desk for three participants is about right. Often on a fine summer day you can have the centre almost to yourself! Some consultancies offering this premier service can provide the executive with his or her own room rather than sharing. An office of your own is certainly standard in continental Europe, where relations are a little more formal.

Another decision to be made when selecting executive services lies in the ambience of the centre. Since fees are high, one should expect a high standard of accommodation. On the other hand, it must not be so comfortable that individuals prefer it to finding a job. Surprising though it may sound, some separation packages are so generous that the fortunate executive can use the centre rather like a club, somewhere to lunch, call stockbrokers and meet friends. The best image I have come across was from an executive who called his centre 'the departure lounge' – clean, efficient, comfortable but really one would prefer to be somewhere else. The questions for the purchaser of outplacement to consider are 'Do I see my people working well in this environment?' and 'Are the facilities what I would need if I was actively job hunting?'

The executive counselling process

The counselling process for executives on a one-to-one basis and the training group method for more junior staff are essentially the same although the level and style of delivery and the time available are more generous in the case of the more senior group. The process is usually along the following lines. An administration form is suggested in fig. 3.

- Initial counselling: gaining biographical data and explaining immediate issues of concern.
- Achievement list: clients write up all the achievements they can think of to do with life and career.
- Management skills inventory: from the achievement list developing a personal portfolio of management and saleable skills.
- Personal profile: developing a statement about oneself in twenty to thirty words about what is being presented to the job market.
- Personal success inventory: those recent or appropriate successes which can be quantified and which support the personal profile.
- Three jobs: development of three possible types of job that can be searched for.
- Psychological assessment: development of a personality profile with a psychologist.
- Development and agreement of CV.
- Identifying job market opportunities.
- Practice interview.
- Draft job search campaign:

PRIVATE AND CONFIDENTIAL

Individual record: .... Name: ....

Contact telephone: ....

Personal data

Home address: Date of birth: .... Age: ....

.... Marital status: ....

.... Children (with ages): 1 ....

.... 2 ....

.... 3 ....

.... 4 ....

Spouse's name: ....

Job history

Releasing organization: ....

Job title: ....

Salary (+ bonus): ....

Date of release: ....

Company contact: ....

Telephone number: ....

Fax number: ....

Counsellors

1 ....

2 ....

3 ....

Psychologist

....

Type of outplacement service contracted: ....

Counselling sessions				*Process stages*	
Date	*Session*	*Duration*	*Counsellor*	*Stage*	*Date*
	1			Achievement list	
	2			Skill profile	
	3			Success inventory	
	4			Three jobs	
	5			Psychological profile	
	6			CV preparation	
	7			CV printed	
	8			Personal campaign	
	9			Headhunter lists	
	10			Practice interview	
	11			Contract negotiation	
	12			Sign off	

Client advised ....

Figure 3. An example of a one-to-one counselling administration form

Personal contacts.
Answering advertisements.
Letters sent 'cold'.
Headhunters.
Prepare for specific interviews.
Counselling on selecting the right offer.
Training in negotiating a contract.
Developing a career plan.
Exit interview and review.

Not all these stages are necessary, nor is it essential to follow them in this sequence. Sometimes people come to the consultancy having already secured interviews, in which case the process outlined above would be almost reversed. Access to the counsellor or the psychologist can take place at any time during the process.

Personal review

This is basically a personal stocktaking exercise, looking at oneself and teasing out strengths and weaknesses. It is sometimes done by the individuals themselves, sometimes completed together with a counsellor. There are various methodologies. Some consultants work on the basis of an individual SWOT analysis (Strengths, Weaknesses, Opportunities and Threats), others develop a huge achievement list where individuals write down as many achievements as they can remember from every aspect of their lives. The latter is particularly cathartic when people's ego is low. Other variations are the lifeline exercises of the type developed by Barrie Hopson and Mike Scally of the Consultancy Lifeskills Associates in Leeds, but all have the aim of assisting individuals to understand themselves and what they can contribute to a future employer. An example is shown below. Such exercises are useful not only in rebuilding a bruised ego but also in providing the basis of information for the CV and the personal curriculum that can be given at interview.

Career influences

- The following events/friends/people have had an effect on

my job decisions (decisions to pursue jobs, give up jobs or make choices about my career) up to now:

	Names/events	*How influenced?*
1	....	....
2	....	....
3	....	....
4	....	....
5	....	....

- The following are my best achievements at work and during my career:

	Names/events	*Skill/talent demonstrated*
1	....	....
2	....	....
3	....	....
4	....	....
5	....	....

- I have done well when I have (related to achievements):

	Names/events	*Reason*
1	....	....
2	....	....
3	....	....
4	....	....
5	....	....

- These are examples of the risks (each job move is a risk) I have chosen to take to further my career:

	Risk	*The pay-off?*
1	....	....
2	....	....
3	....	....
4	....	....
5	....	....

- In my job I got on with others and contributed to their job/personal development in the following ways:

  1 ....
  2 ....
  3 ....
  4 ....
  5 ....

- If a supportive business colleague who knew me well had only thirty words to describe me to a potential employer, he would say:

  ....
  ....
  ....

- If I could have any job in the world it would be ....
  ....

OR

- If money were not important I would want to be ....
  ....
  ....

- If I could describe myself in only three adjectives I would say:

  ....

After Woodcock and Francis (1982); Timm and Peterson (1982); Nelson-Bolles (1989)

Assessment of skills and disposition

During this process of self-discovery the better consultancies also provide psychometric feedback information. This is particularly useful in helping the individual to understand him or herself better. It also provides a vocabulary and information from which they can talk about themselves. A variety of instruments are employed. My own favourites are the MBTI, the 16PF and the OPQ. Each has its own strengths, MBTI being useful for counselling, the 16PF for career themes (see Krug 1981) and OPQ for style of work. Assessments of team role and motivational style have also been used to help people understand themselves and thus be more fluent when talking about their achievements at interview. Should a complete change of career be envisaged, aptitude and interest batteries are used. Where appropriate the individual's values and/or requirements in a career can be assessed through the Repertory Grid system or less thoroughly through an instrument such as the Knowdell Card Set.

Some consultancies employ psychometrics (see p. 90). Learning style questionnaires can be used to understand the individual's likely approach to job search, and the Internal Locus of Control questionnaire will suggest whether the person needs to be pushed or pulled through the transition process. Anyone can put themselves forward to be trained in the administration and interpretation of psychometric material, but the better consultancies will call on chartered psychologists or at least people with an occupational test users' statement or certificate.

Occupational skills inventory

This really arises out of the previous two sections. The individual can now assess what they have achieved in the past and want to achieve in the future, listing the skills and qualities they have available to draw upon.

Getting it down on paper: CV preparation

The CV must fight for attention in the same way as the 'cold' letter. Most executives find the process of writing a CV an incredibly boring chore. They forget that reading sixty or seventy CVs a day, sometimes more, in response to a job advertisement can be even more boring. Job searchers need continual reminding that when it is easier for a recruiter to move on to the next CV he or she will do so. The implication is that all selectors think they are good at what they do. They have to come to that conclusion because they never receive any evidence to the contrary; they never know how good the candidates they have turned down may have been. The difficulty with providing advice, guidance and training on CV preparation is that there are no absolutes. There are no golden rules, only principles. It is a case of getting it right by getting it wrong – seeing what works and what does not work for the individual in the job market.

It is crucial that the individual job searcher feels comfortable with the CV, and so it has to be constructed and written by him or her. The criticism addressed to the counsellor, 'Well, your CV isn't getting me many interviews,' is prevented. Such a remark is a symptom of a deeper problem concerning the relationship between the executive and the counsellor, summed up in the phrase 'What are you doing to help me get my next job?' (See the section on counselling for amplification of the responsibility of individuals for themselves.) An additional difficulty for the released executive is that everyone who sees the CV will express a different viewpoint, revealing their own likes and dislikes in terms of presentation.

The executive is going to be interviewed on the basis of the information and style of the CV. The CV sets up expectations in the mind of the reader. If they are not fulfilled during the interview, even if the candidate is strong and meets the job criteria, it is unlikely that an offer will be made. The CV style must match the person and vice versa.

The overall gauge of what is right or appropriate in a CV must be what works. This is where outplacement can make a significant contribution, since consultants deal with hundreds of executives each year. In what follows some ideas and concepts about CV preparation are put forward. It does not attempt to be a 'How to write a CV' guide, only to give line managers particularly an appreciation of how the construction of CVs has changed over the last decade or so to be more effective.

Types of CV

Chronological
The CV can be written historically, with the following structure:

- Name.
- Address.
- Telephone number.
- Date of birth.
- Marital status.
- Education.
  - School.
  - College.
  - Professional memberships.
- Employment history.
- Interests.

In outplacement terms this is known as the 'tombstone' approach, since it reads like a traditional obituary. An example is shown in appendix 2. Few outplacement consultancies recommend this approach to what is, after all, a personal sales brochure.

Thematic
This is much favoured by the Ministry of Defence and the armed services. As the name suggests, the experience of the job searcher is not ordered chronologically but organized by theme. The structure will be the same as with the chronological style except that the employment history is divided up into themes such as:

- Management.
- Administration.
- Personnel.
- Training.

It is not known why this form of CV is so popular with those who outplace servicemen. Perhaps it is felt that so many tours of duty would be confusing. The record suggests that it is not popular with HR managers because it is difficult to follow and even more difficult to know how recent the experience is.

Achievement
From trial and error in the job market, what has become known as the 'achievement CV' is the form most favoured by outplacement consultancies. The overall structure follows the principles of a sales brochure, providing information in simple, positive statements sequenced for the reader's convenience in reaching a decision. Achievements relevant to the type of position currently being pursued are highlighted and rank-ordered appropriately. Where possible, individuals are encouraged to quantify their achievements in terms of value, size or percentage. This gives far more punch and credibility. If at all possible, the actual benefit to the employer should also be indicated. An achievement CV is shown in appendix 2, where the tombstone style is transformed for direct comparison.

It has now almost become mandatory to use the past tense rather than the abstract noun or participle, e.g. 'managed' is preferable to 'management' or 'managing'.

So achievements might be listed as:

1 Developed a series of . . .
2 Introduced new methods of . . .
3 Organized several . . .

This is thought to generate the idea in the reader's mind, 'Well, if he/she did it for them, he/she can do it for us.' Anyone can hold responsibility but an achievement must mean something was actually done.

The structure of an achievement-oriented CV would be as follows:

- Name.
- Address.
- Telephone number.
- Career statement.
- Career to date (in reverse chronological order).
- Professional qualifications.
- Education.

- Interests.
- Personal details.

Most headhunters and employers wish to see personal details immediately after name and address, but for applicants outside their golden decade – 30–40 for men and in this sexist world 25–35 for women – the results suggest a better response if this information appears towards the end of the CV. Women are far more likely to gain an interview if their marital status is omitted – another sad comment on a sexist employment world.

The impact of the simple strategies can be quite significant, as the examples of a 'before' (chronological) and 'after' (achievement-type) CV demonstrate even for a quite junior management job. It can be seen that the achievement CV features several changes for the better:

- A career statement.
- Reverse chronological career history.
- Achievements are quantified.
- Job title is presented before employer and dates of employment.
- Salary information is omitted.
- Earlier non-relevant experience is condensed.
- A mediocre education is 'hidden'.
- Personal details appear last.

Employers would prefer to have salary information, especially for the last job position. The problem for applicants is that declaring salary information either makes them too expensive when in reality they have no job, or it disadvantages them in negotiating a better salary because they have been forced to reveal their hand.

It is not being suggested that the achievement CV is the best or the only format, but it seems to work better than others in achieving interview opportunities.

How jobs are found

Being shown how the job market works is a major aspect of

the assistance given to everyone who is outplaced in consultancy centres. Basically there are four methods of securing a new job: responding to an advert, going to an agency, gaining a recommendation through a friend, or what is known as 'going cold'. By far the most popular with job seekers are the first two, although all outplacement counsellors know they are the least productive. The figures vary enormously according to circumstances but in very general terms the way individuals secure jobs when supported by outplacement services is divided in the following proportions: 30 per cent by answering advertisements, 15 per cent through agencies, 30 per cent by personal recommendation and 25 per cent by applying 'cold'. It should be noted, though, that with very senior people from the larger blue-chip firms the personal network and 'cold' applications are likely to be considerably more productive than the other two. This is why so many outplacement consultancies talk about the 'unadvertised' job market.

Why individuals should be reluctant to pursue the two more fruitful methods is not clear. Certainly, responding to an advertisement or going to an agency requires less effort. In responding to an advert or going to an agency it is quite clear what has to be done and the procedure is to a certain extent familiar. It has been argued that this approach is favoured because it gives the illusion of choice in that the individual selects the advert or the agency. However, the more convincing explanation is that in networking and going cold there is a high degree of uncertainty which, when one is out of work, is psychologically unattractive. The job seeker has to 'ask' for a job, whereas in adverts and agencies it is the employer who is doing the asking. Many job seekers find it demeaning to ask because it forces them to recognize their unemployed status.

It is sometimes surprising how difficult executives find writing off for jobs, and this is where the adviser can be of enormous assistance. Reflection on the number of executives pursuing the best jobs in the best firms quickly shows how vital it is to produce a simple, effective and interesting letter which stands out, demanding attention. Even more is this true for headhunters, who are swamped daily by unsolicited mail. In my experience it takes, on average, thirty well-constructed 'rifle-shot' cold letters to generate an interview and about five interviews to secure a job. 'Rifle-shot' means identifying, researching and writing to *specific* organizations likely to benefit from the executive's portfolio of skills. The same figures tend to recur whether it is for senior executives or for more junior staff, irrespective of the locality or the local unemployment level. The shotgun approach, that is, writing to all and sundry saying, 'Hire me,' sometimes works but usually does not.

The counsellor can help the individual executive cope with the number of polite turn-downs, or 'thins' (invitations to interview and job offers usually contain additional information and therefore are known as 'fats'). Many organizations and headhunters receive so many cold applications that they no longer reply. For a job searcher who spends hours crafting a batch of, say, twenty letters and does not get one reply it is very frustrating and disappointing. Frequently it takes all the skills of the counsellor to maintain the motivation to work just as hard on the next set of twenty. It is the same with more junior staff and hourly paid employees. To combat despondency job shops give prizes to those who have sent out most cold applications over a period and keep a record of the highest number of applications sent.

There are some general rules for letters. They have to be different, but not so different as to suggest the candidate is a risk; interesting in that the candidate seems worth seeing as a person as well as for what he or she has to offer; finally, the letter should direct the reader to the specific area of the CV which is relevant to the potential employer. David Sagar, a counsellor with Pauline Hyde & Associates, is fond of saying, 'Write a letter which for you is just over the top.' That is to say, slightly more assertive or daring than you would normally write.

- Keep it brief. A wordy covering letter is a positive deterrent to reading the CV.
- Do not be tempted to replicate your CV. The CV is your presentation document and, if composed correctly, will speak for you.
- The letter must be addressed to a specific individual.
- Whether handwritten or typed, it should be signed personally, with your name printed in brackets below the signature.

- Ideally, it will contain three simple paragraphs:

  — The first should begin with 'You' or 'Your' and state the basis of your submission, e.g. 'Your company has announced a new project,' 'has recently advertised vacancies' (don't be specific), 'is expanding rapidly', etc.
  — The second paragraph notes your job search and the enclosure of a CV, e.g. 'I am currently seeking a career move, and enclose my CV.'
  — The third paragraph asks for an informal interview, e.g. 'I would be pleased to visit your offices to discuss the matter further.' You might add here a follow-up suggestion, e.g. 'I hope to hear from you shortly,' or 'I shall contact you shortly to see how matters have progressed.'

- Letters addressed to individuals by name should be signed with 'Yours sincerely', not 'Yours faithfully'.
- If the letter is to be handwritten, ensure it is easily legible.

The following example is the most daring of the more daring letters I have seen. You either hate it or love it but the results were impressive. It was sent just before Easter to headhunters and achieved thirty interviews which led to several job offers.

Dear Mr ——

An Easter egg

An Easter egg is a brightly packaged confectionery that delivers chocolate in an effective and novel way.

I come packaged with an MBA, fluency in German and a rainbow of real-life experience earned with two blue-chip companies.

I have demonstrated a results orientation in new business areas and in developing brand-new marketing opportunities across international markets.

If you have a client company in need of someone who can package and deliver their product or services more effectively, let's discuss.

The better Easter eggs come filled with good things. As an alternative, I enclose my CV.

Yours sincerely

Selling one's self: training in interview skills

If the job market is attacked with vigour and persistence the executive will be rewarded with interviews. The outplacement adviser's key responsibility is to ensure that the individual presents himself in the best way possible, with complete honesty. The majority of managers involved in recruitment have not been trained in interviewing. It is important to ensure that candidates do not take advantage of them and secure jobs for which they are not suited. The skill in outplacement is getting the individual to present himself well and truthfully, not to con his way into a job.

Interview training covers such things as the objectives of the interview, how to create rapport, and how to ensure that the interviewer quickly receives the right impression of the candidate's main skills, achievements and talents. After training in interview skills meetings with potential employers become less like interviews and more like career discussions. The individual is not only presenting his or her competences but matching them up against the requirements of the position vacant.

The candidate is taught the advantages and dangers associated with open questions, and preparation can always be made for the standard questions outlined below.

Achievement questions

- What are you doing best right now?
- What did you do in your last job?
- What would your boss say about your work?
- Why do you think you got that job?
- What was it in your performance that made you a candidate for promotion?
- What are you most proud of in your work?
- What makes you feel you did a good job?
- How has your education helped your career?
- What makes you special and why should we select you?
- What sort of decisions do you take in your job?
- How do you get on with managers/subordinates/colleagues?
- How would a good friend describe you?
- Describe yourself in three words.

- Tell me about an event that challenged you.
- What motivates you?
- What are you looking for in a job?
- How did you get into the field of——?
- What sort of manager are you?

Objections and nasties

- We prefer younger/older people than you.
- Why have you been out of work for so long?
- Why have you changed/stayed in jobs so frequently/long?
- Why is your pay so low, given these achievements in your job history/CV?
- Why were you fired/made redundant/let go?
- Why didn't you do better in that job?
- Why did you fail in that job?
- We prefer more/less experienced people than you.
- I don't think you can do this job.
- What haven't you got for this post?
- How might someone who disliked you describe you?

Weaknesses and failures

- What do you find difficult at work?
- What is the biggest problem at work you have had to overcome?
- If you could change your job what would you do?
- Whom do you find it difficult to work with?
- What is the hardest aspect of your job?
- Given a choice, what things in your job do you leave until later?
- What makes you angry?
- What are you bad at?
- Tell me about a time when you thought you had failed.
- What was your biggest mistake?

Potential

- What do you see as your next job?
- How ambitious are you?
- What would be your ideal job?
- What do you think you can do for us?
- What do you see yourself doing in *x* years' time?

Other favourite questions

- What salary are you looking for?
- Tell me about your health.
- Tell me about your family.
- Tell me about your interests.
- Tell me about your last organization.
- Tell me about your present boss.
- What kind of people do you like to work for/with?
- How did you get that job?

Interviewing sessions are particularly useful because the standard of interviewing skills is very low in Britain. A trained candidate, who has had the advantage of interview grooming, can be a positive help to the line manager who fumbles through this part of the selection process, the trained interviewee actively assisting in the process so that both parties can come to an appropriate decision.

Being interviewed is far more than being able to answer questions. The outplacement counsellor will ensure the candidate fully understands and can manage the whole interview process.

When selecting an outplacement consultancy it is worthwhile asking if the following topic areas will be included to ensure that the interview training is not just limited to an hour's session in front of a closed circuit television:

- How to dress for the interview.
- Rapport and body language.
- Discovering the person specification.
- Researching the major issues to be handled in the job.
- Different types of interview structure, e.g. the seven point plan.

- Handling different types of interviewer.
- How to manage the interviewer and the interview process.
- How to keep the interview positive.
- How to open and close the interview.
- How to manage an aggressive or antagonistic interviewer.

It might be useful for the HR director to sit in on an interview counselling session so that he or she can gain a feel for the expertise within the consultancy in this area. When I have done this, I have actually asked the prospective HR client to take over the interview to give the candidate some true to life experience.

It is interesting that HR directors who are themselves outplacement candidates frequently learn much more about their own interviewing skills development by going through this process. They are certainly more empathetic to interviewees because of it.

The job offers

Selection

Outplacement candidates' activity is usually rewarded by multiple offers and assessment is the next stage of the process. With the counsellor, the individual selects the offer that best promises to fulfil current and future needs. The company prepared to pay the most is not necessarily the first choice. Other factors such as organizational style and career prospects are important.

Because outplacement is about career development, not just about finding a job, a counselling process begins to help the individual to choose the right job. John Flouch, who founded CEPEC, likes to challenge people with the phrase 'What do you want to do for the rest of your life?' The function of the outplacement counsellor is to assist the individual to answer this question for themselves.

Figure 4 is an example of how the jobs on offer can be compared on a factual basis once the question 'What do you want to do with the rest of your life?' has been answered.

Job factors	Ranking	*Rating*			
		Position			
		A	B	C	D
Base salary					
Bonuses					
Profit-sharing					
Stock options					
Benefits: Life assurance Medical cover Disability insurance Pay during illness Housing Preferential mortgage Car Transport costs Credit cards Finance planning Tax assistance Club facilities Holidays Other benefits					
Relocation expenses					
Redundancy/severance pay					
Pension arrangements					
Retirement plans					
Salary increments					
Duties/responsibilities					
Authority/chain of command					
Independence/challenge					
Job security					
Job status					
Interpersonal chemistry					
Management style					
Personal lifestyle					
Promotion potential					
Career path progression					
Personal performance confidence					
Working conditions					
Ease of travelling to work					
Cultural/environmental Cost of living considerations					
Spouse/family convenience					
Educational facilities					
Recreational opportunities					
Civic/cultural/religious needs					
Totals					

Figure 4. Offer comparison chart

Negotiation

This is the final part of the selection process. One of the reasons outplacement is so valuable is that people are usually able to secure a more generous remuneration package than their previous one. Training in the basic techniques of salary and benefit negotiation is quickly absorbed. An increase of around 10 per cent is the most common; my record to date is achieving an increase of 165 per cent for one of my candidates.

Most outplaced executives do not feel they are even in a position to negotiate, nor do they realize how wide the scope is. The iron rule of wages is that employers will only pay the minimum to recruit, retain and motivate. Consequently the individual must negotiate as hard as possible. It is well known that, whatever level you join an organization at, if you start with a poor package the chances are you will remain with a poor package. The agenda for negotiation can include:

Remuneration

- Basic salary.
- Bonus.
- On-Target Earnings (OTE).
- Early review.
- Guaranteed review.
- Guaranteed increase.
- Increase on achievement of targets.
- Increase on completion of probationary period.
- Guaranteed cost of living increases.
- Guaranteed 1st of the year increase.

Benefits

- Pension – company contribution, top-ups, additional voluntary contributions (AVCs).
- Life assurance – multiples of salary.
- Holidays.
- Car – type, size, renewal, private mileage, telephone.
- Medical cover – self, family, London hospital rates.
- Dental cover.
- Mortgage facility.

- Bridging loans.
- Home telephone.
- Guaranteed training each year.
- Sabbatical.
- Professional memberships.
- Membership of clubs.
- Personal expense accounts.

Acceptance

There's many a slip 'twixt cup and lip. Often aspects which are negotiated at interview are subsequently forgotten. Participants are encouraged to confirm their acceptance in writing, mentioning the points agreed, so that, in legal jargon, the terms of employment are 'expressed'. Each item of substance should be touched on briefly and accurately:

Example of a letter of acceptance

Dear Mr James

It was a pleasure meeting you last Thursday. This is to confirm my acceptance of the position of HR Director.

I am pleased that I shall be reporting direct to you but for functional and policy arrangements to the European HQ in Geneva.

As my conditions of employment were discussed with a series of company officers over several interviews, it may be helpful if I summarize my understanding of what has been agreed.

Initial salary: £*x*,000 per annum, with an annual review at each anniversary of my starting date.

Bonus: up to 15 per cent, with a minimum of not less than £3,000 per annum.

Profit sharing: whatever distributed.

Stock option programme after one year of service, with an entitlement to acquire 500 shares per year of the Ordinary stock at the prevailing market value less 2 per cent for a period of seven years.

BUPA: for self and family at London teaching hospital rate.

Life assurance: salary × 3.

Pension: 4 per cent contribution by self, 9 per cent by the company.

Car, 2.8 l car, fully serviced, renewable every two years.

Executive outplacement after one year's service should I be released for whatever reason.

Performance review after the first six months and on satisfactory performance an increase in both responsibilities and remuneration.

Thank you for agreement to pick up my direct accommodation expenses for the first ten weeks of my employment and for the advantage of the company's relocation package.

Thank you for your decision and your support. I look forward to reporting to you at 8.30 a.m. on 1 June.

Yours sincerely

____________________________.

Chapter 6

What happens in outplacement (2) services for staff and hourly paid

Sometimes it is necessary for reasons of status to provide different types of outplacement support for different grades of employee. Executives may have one-to-one counselling at a centre, senior managers a five-day programme at an exclusive hotel, junior managers a three-day programme off-site and all others a two-day programme on-site. Outplacement consultancies can advise and can be quite creative around a set budget. Outlined here are the main outplacement provisions that are currently being provided at the less senior level, particularly training and job shops. As with executive services, there are examples and illustrations to assist understanding rather than any attempt to write a manual on how to deliver outplacement to this category of staff.

Group training in job search skills is used when there are large numbers of people being released. Matters which are common to all participants such as CV preparation and interview skills can be covered *en masse*. In a close-down situation some organizations provide training only, some just a job shop, some both. The consultancy can advise on what is best in a particular situation. My own view is that a job shop does not become necessary until about 100 people are being released at any one time. Up to that number can be adequately covered by training provisions but successful job shops have been run for as few as twenty-five people. Usually a budget constraint is the determining factor. Some firms like to have all those being released seen on a one-to-one basis first, to quantify needs before providing training or setting up a job shop.

In order to be effective, job shops must run for at least four weeks. Anything less is scarcely worth the investment in time or fees. It takes a week to identify jobs and another three to service employees. At a minimum that is twenty consultant days. In equivalent training-cum-counselling days a lot more could be done in the same time for much the same fee. One advantage of the job shop is that the employer is seen to be doing something for the released employees. It can send a signal to those who remain. Off-site outplacement counselling or training, whilst more effective in terms of securing jobs, does not provide the same high profile of care.

A good way of testing the competence of an outplacement consultancy is to furnish the number and status of those being released, outline the main reasons and invite the consultancy to propose a menu of services. The better consultancies will be able to put forward a plan tailored to the specifics of the situation. When British Aerospace closed a site employing 4,000 people in Weybridge, training in groups of fifteen was felt not to be as appropriate as an extensive job shop with special training day facilities. GTE, releasing fifteen of its accounts department from one of its sites in Wiltshire, would have been unwise to attempt a job shop. For Hagglunds Denison, closing an engineering factory in Sussex with 150 people, a combination of training and job shop was appropriate.

Typical group programme structures

The overall structure of group programmes, whether for one, two or up to five days' duration, is essentially the same in both process and content. On the longer courses there is more time for individual work and group discussion, whereas the shorter ones tend to be more formal and structured. My own view is that programmes of less than two days cannot be effective. Outplacement training is unlike all other in-company training in that most of the participants are in a state of high anxiety and often anger. It takes time for emotional issues to be resolved before content matters such as CV preparation or job search can be covered. Since it is the most junior staff who get the shortest period of training it could be said that this level of employee needs at least two days to absorb the information. Finally, whilst there is outplacement content which is common to all, such as interviewing, each person comes with his or her own concerns and agenda. There is just not time to tackle them in a one-day session, nor is one day long enough for credibility and trust in the counsellor to be built up among the participants.

The structure of outplacement training reflects the typical product sales structure:

- Product indentification.
- Sales literature.
- Marketing.
- Sales opportunities.
- Brochure development.
- Market planning.
- Publicity campaign.
- Sales presentation.
- Closing and taking the order.

Converting this into outplacement terms, the curriculum of a typical programme would be:

- Self-review: a historical and present SWOT analysis.
- Career opportunities.
- CV writing.
- Self-marketing to:

  Agencies.
  Adverts.
  Network opportunities.
  Cold opportunities.

- Interviewee skills and personal grooming.
- Rate or remuneration negotiation.
- Offer selection.

If there is more time it may be possible to include psychometrics, career counselling and closed-circuit television work for interviews.

As can be seen, this structure and sequence are not dissimilar to those provided to executives. Here they are more structured, formalized and prescriptive. Counselling style, if any, tends to be more direct or at least strategic. One of the costs of training in outplacement programmes is that individuals have to be processed rather than non-directly counselled, and individual concerns and issues are not always resolved satisfactorily.

However, group training does offer some advantages over

one-to-one. Just as in group therapy strength and encouragement can be gained from knowing that you are not alone and that others suffer the same difficulties, so in group outplacement individuals are often relieved that others feel just as angry or depressed. There are benefits in mutual resourcing and job hunting: it can become less lonely, more competitive, even fun in pairs or groups where individuals can gain from the support of others. At Britoil in Scotland a group of released executives continued to gather long after they had all found jobs. The regular meetings were so useful that they formed an Action Learning Set for their new careers.

Some of the large one-to-one outplacement consultancies have realized the benefits of group work and put their clients into co-counselling or triad sets where two or three people work together on their job hunts. A way of looking at the training is in terms of a job search spiral (fig. 5), moving from self-assessment to career optioning through job search skill and job search action, which concludes when new employment is found.

In the early 1980s, John Talbot of EMAS Consultants pioneered group outplacement schemes using an Action Learning model. His design would be an initial training session of two to five days, with one-day follow-up meetings for the groups at monthly intervals thereafter. For the participants this assisted motivation and mutual support, for employers it provided better evaluation of progress and results, and for consultancies it was an opportunity to do a better job (though of course at a higher fee). Most consultancies use Talbot's structure in one way or another because it has proved so successful.

Job shops and resource centres

A job shop is essentially the same concept as a high street Job Centre but with a very significant difference. A Job Centre is reactive to enquiries, whilst a job shop is proactive: it scours the travel-to-work area for job opportunities for those who are being released. This difference is considerable in its effects. A telephone job searcher making anything up to 140 cold calls a day will soon find every local job opportunity there is,

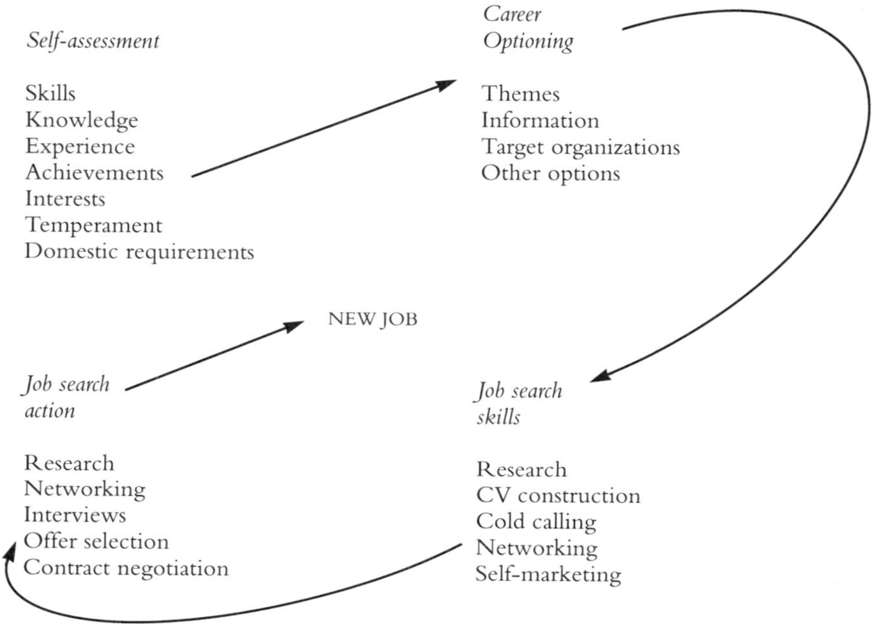

Figure 5. The job spiral

particularly if there are four or five telephone searchers at the start of a project to build up a 'bank' of vacancies.

The job shop brings advantages to all. Those who are leaving receive substantial help. The organization manifests its commitment. Local employers get the benefit of a free recruitment service and the consultancy running the job shop has PR exposure and a physical resource it can show to potential clients. During its lifetime the job shop goes through three distinct phases which have implications for its resourcing.

In the first phase there is a tremendous interest and when it opens everyone will visit it out of curiosity. Conflict between local management and the consultancy may occur if management wish to bring the opening date forward soon after the consultants arrive. The consultancy will not want to open until they have had enough time to ensure that there is a reasonable number of suitable jobs.

The expectation of the released employees will be that the consultants come with a ready-made portfolio of jobs and put pressure on the management to open. Consequently manning at the 'front end' has to be much higher in terms of counsellors and telephone job searchers. Some consultancies manage this initial surge of interest by arranging one-to-one interviews with those immediately affected. Another way is to arrange 'tours' of the job shop at set times so that chaos on the opening day is avoided.

Job shops are still a new enough phenomenon to be of interest to the local press, especially if the consultancy can write some reasonable copy, provide photographs and place some advertising directed at local employers. On some projects there has been an official opening by an appropriate dignitary. This works well when the downsizing is going to extend over a considerable period of time.

The second phase will be the business of matching people to jobs, arranging interviews and giving last-minute support and encouragement. Training in CV preparation and interview techniques is usually given outside the shop. All those affected will need help in these areas and are better dealt with in group sessions.

The last phase will be spent dealing with people who are encountering difficulties in getting a job. The placement of individuals typically follows the S-shape curve shown in fig. 6. In the first phase 20 per cent get jobs slowly as the shop gathers momentum; then in the second phase a further 60 per cent are placed reasonably quickly. The last 20 per cent are the most difficult because they will be the ones who are older, more specialist, have particular requirements or do not fit the structure of the local job market. It is this last 20 per cent who change the nature of the work to a counselling rather than an administrative-cum-training role.

Manning the job shop

Naturally the consultancy would like the client to have as many counsellors as possible, and the higher the ratio of counsellors to releasees the better the service will be (but the higher the fees). The general rule is one counsellor to every 75–100 people released, but with no fewer than two counsel-

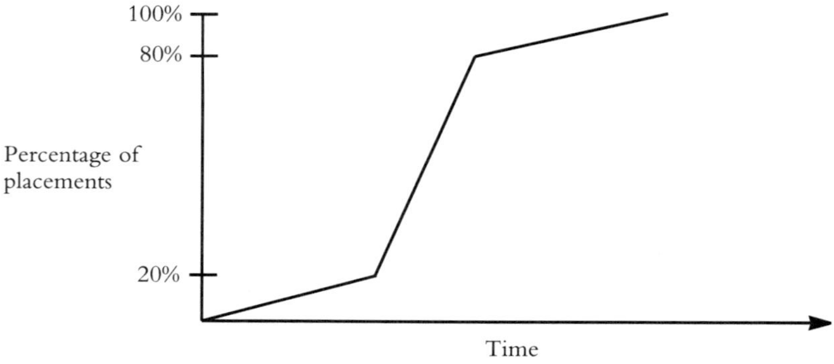

Figure 6. The S-curve of job placements

lors on-site, especially during the first two weeks.

On opening there should be something like 300–500 jobs on display. In a district where unemployment is 6 or 7 per cent it would take three telephone locators five to seven days' calling to identify that number of opportunities. Once the initial bank of jobs has been built up, only one telephone job searcher will be required to 'top up' on a regular basis and check that vacancies are still live. In large downsizings there may need to be a job shop manager or regular visits from a project manager, possibly even regular visits from a specialist counsellor to work with those who have special needs such as anxiety or depression.

Physical resources for the job shop

First it is important for the job shop to be situated where people normally pass by in their daily routine. If placed away from the centre of activity it is easy for a job shop to become marginalized or regarded as a leper colony. If it is central then it is easy for people to get to it. Line management prefer this too, because they know where their people are and, if necessary, chase them back to work.

The job shop itself requires four distinct operational areas. First, a reception area where people can be logged in. It is important to know who comes in and when the most popular times are. Ideally the secretary or receptionist should be somebody popular who knows everybody and what the official and unofficial systems are. In the early stages a known face ensures a greater number of visits, for some are always shy.

The next area required is space to display jobs, opportunities, research material and posters, with tables and chairs for people to sit and read, research and chat. It should be informal, relaxed and comfortable but more like a departure lounge than a waiting room. It should give the feel of a place where things happen. It should also be professional rather than clinical, user-friendly rather than formal. Job shops always attract 'hangers-on' and these have to be chased back to work regularly.

A private area for counselling purposes is essential. Here it is important to ensure confidentiality. Job loss frequently brings personal problems to the fore so people need to know they will not be overheard. Shop stewards in particular may be compromised, on the one hand doing their best to fight the redundancies but on the other needing just as much support as anyone else.

A place for the job searchers, who usually work better together than separately, is the final area. Making one call after another can get tedious but in groups impromptu team games and competitions can be played to keep up motivation and ensure that daily call targets are hit.

Display arrangements

Not surprisingly, job searchers are exceptionally competitive about career opportunities and consequently it is useful to display only job details, pay and hours on the job card, with a code number. This ensures that employees have to see a counsellor before pursuing an opening. In one case where cards displayed all the information some enterprising person on the night shift stole them all to give himself a head start.

Using different colours and different boards enables the details to be displayed attractively by function or locality. A display of 'Today's jobs' is always popular. Local Job Centres are usually most helpful and will pass on details of vacancies they have been invited to fill. These usually take the form of computer print-outs. Should an employee express interest, an interview is arranged through the Job Centre. Other displays can be the appointment pages of the local papers and appropriate journals as well as location and travel maps of the catchment area.

An essential display is the results of the job shop, which can include:

- Number of jobs discovered cold (actual).
- Number of interviews secured (actual).
- Highest number of cold calls made by an individual.
- Highest number of interviews achieved.
- Highest salary gain achieved.
- Highest number of offers achieved.
- Best benefits achieved.

When outplacement training is being provided, it is helpful and supportive to display the route through which the jobs have been achieved, namely agency, advertisement, network or cold. A pie chart displaying the various percentages of jobs achieved via each category will demonstrate how effective networking and cold calling can be.

Visits

It is important to keep interest in the job shop fresh. Posters and layout need changing regularly and every job display should look live and real. Additional interest is created by arranging talks and presentations on related topics by organizations such as:

- DSS: benefits and how to claim.
- Independent financial organizations.
- Local colleges.
- Recruitment agencies.
- Local employers.
- Local Training Education Councils.
- Banks, building societies and insurance agents.
- Dress and make-up advisers.

Job shop hours

As part of being user-friendly it is important for the job shop to be open when people find it convenient, which is usually before or at the end of a shift. If it is double-day or triple-shift working the opening hours should not favour any one shift. In my experience the night shift usually feel left out, so extra provision here is always well received.

Control mechanisms

Job shops are usually provided in situations where there are phased reductions in manpower. This means that during the operation of the job shop normal standards of output will still be required. It is important not to antagonize line management by encouraging visits when employees have other commitments. Line management can sabotage a job shop by making it impossible for employees to visit. Hence arrangements about release time and duration of visits need to be agreed beforehand.

Employees have a right to reasonable time off work to look for employment. With forethought and planning it is possible to ensure that, when interviews are arranged, it is with minimum disruption of manufacturing or work commitments. Co-operation between line managers and job shop will ensure that one is not played off against the other.

The client also needs to know about job shop usage and success rates. Figures 7–8 show an actual example of a simple control mechanism for information which is kept on a daily basis. Averages are useful for identifying deviations or new trends. Better still is the use of the standard deviation, any change in which should be investigated.

Date: .... Week commencing: ....

STATISTICS

Total of telephone contacts made ....

Total of new vacancies raised ....

Number visiting job shop ....

Number counselled for all purposes ....

Number of employers contacted by phone ....

Number of employers contacted by letter ....

Number of employers visiting job shop ....

Number of employers selection interviews ....

Number of placements ....

WORKSHEET

Counselled (all categories)	*Telephone contacts*	*Telephone jobs*

OTHER CONTACTS, INITIATIVES, ETC.

Figure 7. Example of a daily return for a job shop

DAILY REPORT

Date	Calls made	Total	Jobs	to date	Visits	Counselled	Interviews	Placements	Action
$\bar{X}$	130		19		125	25	3.2	3	
4/9	138	4293	18	960	95	31/2427	7	8/67	
7/9	118	4411	17	977	133	30/2457	2	0/67	
8/9	214	4625	10	987	189	13/2570	2	1/68	★
9/9	159	4784	25	1012	103	15/2585	4	0/68	
10/9	169	4953	18	1020	192	10/2595	0	0/68	
11/9	157	5110	30	1050	97	13/2608	0	31/99	★
14/9	164	5274	56	1106	97	25/2633	2	1/100	
15/9	165	5439	9	1115	214	52/2685	22	1/101	★★
16/9	87	5526	16	1131	111	50/2735	2	0/101	–
17/9	122	5648	11	1142	165	47/2782	3	39/140	★
18/9	152	5800	33	1175	109	40/2822	1	0/140	
21/9	116	5916	13	1188	139	31/2853	5	0/142	
22/9	89	6005	16	1204	182	32/2885	2	2/145	–
23/9	114	6119	12	1216	95	14/2899	1	3/145	
24/9	104	6223	9	1225	157	15/2914	2	0/145	★ –
25/9	66	6289	22	1247	40	14/2928	1	1/146	
$\bar{X}$	133		20		132	27	3.5	5.5	

Figure 8. Example of a daily log sheet for a job shop

Chapter 7

Post-outplacement issues

The survivor syndrome, or bail-out phenomenon

When people are released there is a direct effect on those who stay. This is not always recognized by those who manage the downsizing, yet the way it is done can have a lasting effect on the rest of the organization. People who are made redundant can give vent to their feelings. Good outplacement makes provision for the release of emotions but there are no such facilities for those who stay.

In 1988 Dr David Lane, supported by Coutts Career Consultants, undertook research with a sample group of fifty senior and middle managers whose peer groups had experienced significant redundancies. Of the executives retained in the six organizations surveyed, one in five subsequently left because of the way the restructuring had been managed. It was a question not so much of what happened as of how. They recognized the need for restructuring; nevertheless, those who went had been friends, colleagues, part of their lives. If those who are released feel bereaved, not dissimilar feelings are experienced by those who remain.

Once an organization has made people redundant the essential element of trust on the part of employees is lost, and it takes considerable time before it can be rekindled. Relief which is felt by those who keep their jobs quickly turns to guilt because the relief is caused by a friend's misfortune. And the uncertainty of 'It may be my turn next time' will linger. For some people this cocktail of emotions can be purged only by seeking a position elsewhere. This is the 'survivor syndrome' at its worst – what the Americans call the bail-out phenomenon. It can cost the company dear, particularly in acquisitions when it is essential to the acquirer that key players should remain in place. Thus there is a role not only for outplacement counselling but also for 'inplacement' counselling for those who stay.

Post-outplacement activities

Just as it is important to manage the front end of the merger, acquisition or downsizing, it is also important to manage the back end. Often the post-outplacement situation is just as difficult. It involves overcoming the 'us and them' anxieties, power aspirations on the part of newly positioned executives, bail-outs and dips in performance that nearly always accompany a new situation. Inordinate length of time may be needed for the new organization to settle down. If management does nothing to accelerate the development of a new culture and vision the period of corporate lethargy or drift is both longer and more costly.

Affirmations that 'all is well and all will be well' are not sufficient. Management's credibility at such times is usually, in my experience, at a low ebb. Coming at the reorganization crisis for the first time, managements usually get it right by first getting it wrong and then making adjustments. Release dates get put back or brought forward, organization structures are changed and changed again, reporting relationships alter. Even people who are released get taken back on again. For all these reasons it is not surprising that when a senior manager addresses the troops on how good the future will be, the best response that can be hoped for is 'We'll see' rather than acceptance.

Communication

Most senior managements fail to appreciate that during the reorganization and immediately after it there is so much ignorance, insecurity and rumour that existing communication arrangements are inadequate to cope with the demand for information. During the initial stages of downsizing, much of the planning, tactics and negotiation necessarily goes on behind closed doors. Employees sense that something is afoot, yet are met with denials and assurances that 'no plans have been made at this moment in time'. This breeds tremendous insecurity. Decisions are made about employees with minimum consultation. Employees find it difficult to 'buy into' the new set-up when they have had no chance to participate in its formation. In the post-outplacement phase, decisions should be made wherever possible with maximum employee participation.

The information that is required falls into three categories:

- Information on the merger, acquisition or downsizing. Who is doing what, why, the result and when.
- Information on what work has to be done for their unit or department.
- How and when the changes are likely to affect individuals and their work.

Giving the bad news well is even more important than conveying good news. People need to know where they stand. In such situations there is an information vacuum. If management do not fill it with solid fact it will be filled by rumour and hearsay, most of it as negative as it is fantastic. It was rumoured in one small Yorkshire printing firm that the doomed business was going to be acquired by an incredibly wealthy Indian princess, and she was going to ensure that all the jobs were preserved. The only conceivable basis for the story was that just before the announcement of closure the general manager had been visited by a smartly dressed female Indian accountant from the firm's London auditors. Someone had put two and two together and made five. In another close-down Lord Lucan was said to have had a major interest!

Inaccurate information is just as dangerous as no information. It is better for management to get up and say 'We have no information' than to fudge or filibuster. What is said and done at such a time by senior management is interpreted as evidence of what the organization is going to be like in the future.

Written communications

A special news-sheet or house journal which has the same duration as the merger or acquisition is a good way of giving out formal information and is useful as a subsequent source of reference. A section can be given over to 'Questions and answers' and another to employee comments or observations.

Help lines

This is useful not only in facilitating an instant response to employees' queries and concerns but also in indicating what the issues are which can furnish the content of future issues of a news-sheet. Rather like customer care, if one person has an issue which needs to be resolved that person is probably speaking for ten or more others with a similar concern.

Formal meetings

In addition to the presentation of information, formal meetings, gatherings or road shows provide an opportunity for employees to voice their opinions. Again, information which bubbles up at these meetings can be thought through and addressed in the next edition of the fact sheet or house journal.

Workshops and open seminars

These can do a great deal to help integrate two new groups of people as well as providing an opportunity to focus on likely difficulties and conflict. In the US, UNISYS devised a series of workshops specifically to address the problems people were experiencing or expecting. It has always surprised me that no British outplacement consultancies have extended their services to cater for this very important niche of the market. The curriculum of such meetings, possibly led by an outsider to eliminate any source of bias, could be along the lines of:

- What were the good things about our separate cultures (or the way they were before the downsizing)?
- What would we like to change in our culture now that we have the opportunity?
- In terms of culture what would we like our new organization to be?
- Where do we foresee difficulties in the immediate future and what ideas have I for resolving them?
- How can we work better together, preserve the best of the past and make the most of the future?

Workshops addressing these ideas will do much to improve

relations and understanding. They will be particularly useful after a merger or acquisition, but they will work just as well post-downsizing.

Team-building activities

In the 1960s researchers discovered that when new groups or teams are brought together they go through a process of 'storming, norming, conforming and performing'. That is to say, before they can co-operate effectively they need to discover how to relate to each other. Each member of the team has to discover what other members will and will not do, and how they react in different situations. This is the storming phase. What is learnt here is translated into informal rules of social interaction – the norming phase. Then the group can invest time and effort in maintaining 'the way things are done round here', which is the conforming phase. It is only when these phases have been worked through that the group can perform effectively.

Team events can accelerate this consolidation process. In addition time can be consciously spent on developing a vision of the future and mutual commitment to achieving it. As part of the curriculum for the team, events can be based on a tripartite approach along the following lines.

- *Imagery*. How do members see each other? What stereotypes are there? What are the myths and stories about the merging or acquiring firm? What are the fears about the new structure?
- *Confrontation*. Work on the recognition of the differences between group members and how they might or might not be useful in the new situation. (If the differences are not recognized and voiced, acceptance and resolution become difficult.)
- *Bonding*. The team can agree on how best to manage the present and future objectives, realizing (*a*) where they might experience conflict, (*b*) where others in the group are coming from, (*c*) what levels of skill and expertise are in the group, (*d*) how it will be possible to work together.

In this way the three important aspects of team effectiveness can be maximized; goals can be set, processed and recognized; and personal relationships can blossom.

Employee support counselling

Some employees encounter difficulties adjusting to the new culture or their new role and could benefit from counselling in making the transition to the rigours of the new environment. Personal success is a combination of ability, motivation and circumstances, and what sometimes happens is that individuals are surprised when what they do or the way they do it no longer works. Rather than change their tactics they try harder and become confused when even the greater effort is not successful. Counselling to help the individual appreciate the different requirements of the new situation can be beneficial.

Other employees may have difficulty coping with their new position or with greater responsibilities. The new conditions usually bring with them more testing demands. Counselling can help the individual deal with the stress of the situation and develop new strategies for managing both new role and workload.

Employee questionnaires

This is the established way of testing attitudes and feelings. Questionnaires provide the organization with a baseline of information. If the questionnaire is repeated after a suitable interval the shift in attitudes or feelings can be, if not measured, at least identified. Likely danger areas or trouble spots can be highlighted, as well as the impact other initiatives, such as team events, have on a particular department or unit. Special areas requiring extra care and attention can also be identified.

The topics for an employee questionnaire in a post-merger, acquisition or downsize situation could usefully include:

- Management style.
- Job satisfaction.
- Personal stress.
- Job relations with co-workers and/or other units.
- Organization of work and work flow.

It should be remembered that employee surveys generate high expectations among those who complete them that:

- The results will be published quickly.
- The results will be made available to all who participated.
- Management action will follow.

If the purpose is to get a 'before and after' picture, the above actions must be seen to be effective after the first questionnaire, otherwise individuals will not co-operate with – or, more likely, will be deviant in their completion of – the second or 'after' questionnaire. For more detailed guidance on conducting successful employee surveys read *What about the Workers?: making employee surveys work* (Walters 1990).

Promotional material

Promotional material can be used in the new organization, treating employees as if they were customers needing to be told that there are not two companies but one. At SmithKline Beecham 'Now we are one' coffee mats began to appear, gradually emigrating to all the UK plants. Promotional items such as T shirts, hats, pens and the like are less common this side of the Atlantic but nevertheless, with thought, can be used to endorse or underpin the corporate message about the new situation.

It was as a result of a competition among the employees that the name *UNISYS* itself was coined. It is rumoured that in the US employees had hats with both Sperry and Burroughs on them which were replaced with new ones lettered UNISYS. Should a manager or executive act in a way reminiscent of either the Burroughs or the Sperry tradition he or she was told to wear the new corporation hat.

Induction

It is important that new employees are oriented towards values of the future rather than being reminded how much better things were in the 'good old days'. New employees not party to the old traditions are useful in the integration process, often pointing out to existing employees that retrospection is inappropriate when there is so much to go for. Most induction programmes emphasize the history of the organization for the new employee. In post-merger or acquisition situations the future vision and goals need to assume the greater significance. Care also needs to be taken that those who handle outplacement are equally committed to the new rather than projecting a partisan or retrospective viewpoint.

Each post-downsizing situation is different and no one approach or technique will be sufficient to create acceptance, integration and commitment to the new environment. In my experience management are great at the 'front end' of outplacements but assume that it will all come right at the 'back end'.

Certainly managers will be expending additional effort to make the new organization work, preserve existing clients and generate new ones as well as securing their own future. Consequently the human issues are frequently overlooked. Employees working in unfamiliar conditions such as those due to merger or acquisition cannot give of their best. To be effective, especially where complete integration is called for, an understanding of the process issues is paramount and anything that assists integration should be championed.

Conclusion

Outplacement is a significant human resource activity calling upon knowledge and skills from every aspect of the personnel profession. It requires a good knowledge of industrial relations law – particularly the law relating to contracts and redundancy – to ensure that individuals receive, at least, their statutory rights and entitlements. The strategy requirements of downsizing, merger or acquisition demand management skills of the highest calibre, particularly when the interests of the business need to be balanced against the moral imperatives of releasing employees and all the hardships, both actual and psychological, that entails. To assist the individual in any meaningful way takes counselling and training skills of the highest order. Career decisions taken under the care of outplacement counsellors are for most individuals among the most significant of their lives. For the same reason training skills have to be excellent. Training groups of hourly paid employees is just as important as assisting an ex-managing director through his or her career choice. The implications are awesome for the individual trainees and thereby the consultants who deliver the programmes.

Consequently, the choice of outplacement consultancy is crucial. I hope that in this book I have contributed in some small way to make this choice more informed so that *all* parties benefit – those who decide and arrange for people to be made redundant, those whose jobs become redundant and those whose privilege it is to serve them.

Max, it was great. They asked me all the questions you said they would. It was like having all the trump cards in my hand and knowing I couldn't fail.

Safety manager

It's going great. I've got five offers so far and I think I'm going for ten.

Maintenance manager

I didn't believe it when you said I'd earn more. I still can't believe I've got twice as much as I had before.

Financial accountant

It's wonderful. I've got this super job working in a bank. I never dreamed I'd get the office job I always wanted.

Warehouse assistant

I wouldn't want to go through it again but I've learnt so much about myself and my abilities. For the first time in my life I'm in control.

Geologist

Just to let you know that my business has taken off beyond all our wildest dreams. £250,000 worth of contracts in the first two months.

Computer specialist

I lost a job but found a career.

Director

If I'd known this twenty years ago I'd have been successful.

Army major-general

Appendix 1

Example of a redundancy policy

Security of employment agreement

Definitions

(a) *The company*. The Company is defined as the Goodyear Tyre & Rubber Company (Great Britain) Limited, Wolverhampton.

(b) *Goodyear Joint Trade Union Council*. A council has been formed from representatives of ASTMS/AUEW/EETPU and the Engineering Foremen Association with the purpose of arriving at a Security of Employment Agreement with the company and maintaining this agreement. This council may be called together by either party on matters relating directly to this agreement.

The Goodyear Joint Trade Union Council will be convened at the request of either party when any matters of a common interest are to be discussed.

(c) *Volunteer*. A volunteer is an employee who is not identified within a redundancy situation, but is willing to accept the redundancy terms.

(d) *Compulsory*. A compulsorily redundant employee is one whose job title has had surpluses declared under a redundancy situation and has been identified individually within the job classification in accordance with the procedure outlined within this agreement.

Any employee classified as compulsorily redundant will, subject to the conditions of the recall register, be considered for re-engagement.

(e) *Company service*. The current period of continuous employment with the Goodyear Tyre & Rubber Company.

1.0 *Preamble*

1.1 *Management and trade union objectives*

The management and the joint council have an obligation to provide a working partnership which will give the business the best opportunity to provide continuity of employment with the company for all qualified, well trained and motivated employees. In those circumstances, where the business can no longer accommodate such continuity, management and the joint council will practise a fair and consistent approach to all problems.

1.2 The business has to be effective, efficient and competitive in order that its financial performance is satisfactory. The management and the joint council accept that their joint objective should be to achieve the viability and profitability of the business.

1.3 The joint council agrees that the management has to carry out its obligation to improve costs by whatever means practical; but in principle, involvement of the employee and joint council during the decision-making process will be sought.

1.4 Should adverse changes in the fortunes of the business occur it may, from time to time, regrettably make 'redundancy' unavoidable.

This agreement is designed to handle those arrangements for employees whose jobs are surplus to requirements and who are subsequently declared redundant.

1.5 This agreement does not take away management's obligation to consult and discuss change in accordance with its agreements with the joint council.

2.0 *Manpower planning and security of employment*

2.1 An essential part of the company's manpower policy concerns manpower planning and budgeting – this involves the assessment of the business needs with regard to the numbers and quality of the people required. The trade unions agree that management has to ensure that the right balance of skills exists at all levels of the structure to meet the normal present and future business requirements.

2.2 The joint council agrees with the company's objective to try, wherever possible, to develop people from within the company to positions of greater responsibility. Security of employment for the individual will be enhanced by all supporting this objective. However, such an objective does not alter the management's right to hire employees from outside the company where it is considered appropriate and necessary.

2.3 The joint council and the company agree to people in one skill being trained for other skills in accordance with the needs of the business.

The joint council will give help to management by advising people to transfer to suitable alternative employment rather than accepting redundancy where alternative employment exists.

2.4 Adverse change in the business situation will inevitably result in manpower surpluses which cannot be handled by retraining and redeployment. In these situations, management agrees to give consideration to alternative courses of action to give equitable treatment to those employees affected.

3.0 *Manpower surplus*

3.1 The company and the joint council accept that, where a manpower surplus exists, management will identify the surplus jobs in terms of numbers and title within the divisions involved.

3.2 Management will assess the likely duration of the surplus jobs in light of business plans and employee wastage and will review all pertinent business and commercial factors.

3.3 Management will also consider:

- A reduction in overtime working.
- Introducing short-time working.
- Reducing or eliminating the use of temporary, agency or contract workers.
- Curtailing or halting recruitment in the categories of employees affected.
- Transferring employees to suitable alternative work, preferably within the division involved.

- Retraining employees in new skills within the division involved.
- Transferring employees to jobs in other grades in order to maintain job security.
- Transferring employees to other trade groups within the joint council.

3.4 Management will consider the transfer of individuals in surplus jobs to vacancies which exist in other divisions, even where such a move would be considered a 'demotion'. Any such transfer will be conditional on the surplus employee possessing the necessary skills, qualifications and experience for the vacant position.

3.5 If the measures outlined do not succeed in absorbing the manpower surplus then the joint council and management will apply the redundancy process.

4.0 *Consultation*

4.1 The management is committed to keeping the joint council informed about the status of the business. Through this process of communication and consultation, the business performance will be known and understood. This knowledge will give the warning of impending manpower surpluses. (The informal consultation.)

4.2 Management's responsibility is to continually examine the various trends within the business and assess their implications – when the trends are such that some action is believed to be required, management will consult the joint council and inform it of the possible action required to overcome the problem. (The formal dialogue prior to any announcement of surplus jobs.)

4.3 Management will inform the joint council where a surplus exists, giving the following information:

- The reasons for the manpower surplus and the need for redundancies.
- Number and description of jobs it is proposed to discuss as redundant.
- The method of selection.
- The method of carrying out any reductions.
- The key dates for the reductions.

- Whether or not a possibility will exist of volunteers for redundancy being considered. This will depend on the type of job declared surplus and the employee/management structure in the particular department or division.
- List of volunteers.

4.4 The management will give careful consideration to any items raised by the joint council.

5.0 *The redundancy process*

5.1 The joint council representatives initially will be informed, prior to any other employees' communication, about the measures which have been taken to absorb the surplus manpower and the reasons why redundancy was the only alternative. Management will give the numbers and categories of surplus jobs involved and the method to be used to identify those who are involved.

5.2 Decisions on redundancy will be governed primarily by the needs of the business.

The criteria for the selection of those to be made redundant will be determined by the appropriate divisional head in conjunction with Personnel Division and management agrees to take particular note of:

- Agency personnel.
- Twilight shift workers.
- Part-time workers.
- Contractors.
- Temporary hires.
- Employees who are eligible for early retirement.
- Volunteers (acceptable to management) within the defined job categories.
- Short-service rather than long-service employees. However, the following items will be taken into consideration, e.g.:
  - — Attendance records (including absenteeism/timekeeping).
  - — Job performance.
  - — Employee skills (practical and/or academic).
  - — Experience.
  - — Disciplinary records.

The above list is not exhaustive and any consideration will be based on records that were noted and that the employee was aware of at the time of occurrence.

5.3 Management will give warning of redundancies to the appropriate office of the Department of Employment.

5.4 *Procedure and timing*

5.4.1 Management will inform the joint council and employees of the needs and reasons for redundancies.

Day 1

5.4.2 Management/joint council meetings to discuss the best way to achieve the reductions.

Days 1 to 4

5.4.3 Management communicates its decision to the joint council and all employees. HRI notice given to the Department of Employment.

Day 5

5.4.4 List of jobs surplus to requirements published. Initially handed to union officers and then to employees.

Day 5

5.4.5 Notice of selection for redundancy served on employees.

Day 6

5.4.6 Formal notice of termination of employment served on employees.

Day 20

5.4.7 All employees within programme exited.
Date to be given by management.

6.0 *Specific warnings to individual employees*

6.1 The individual employees affected will be advised of their selection for redundancy by their departmental manager and the date upon which the notice of the termination of employment will start.

The 'advice of selection for redundancy' will be for as long a period as possible and in any event will be for a minimum of one calendar week.

6.2 The 'advice of selection for redundancy' will give any employee the right to bring to the attention of management the fact that they feel they have been 'unfairly selected for redundancy'. The procedure for handling redundancy issues will apply, see appendix, paragraph E.

6.3 At the end of the 'advice of selection for redundancy' period, employees will be given their individual notice of termination of employment for reasons of redundancy. The notice period will be in accordance with the entitlement due under current legislation.

6.4 Employees who are declared redundant may request to leave the company during the 'advice of selection for redundancy' period. Management will make every effort to release such employees, who will receive their full redundancy and in-lieu-of-notice payments in accordance with their age and service.

6.5 Employees may also request to leave during their notice of termination of employment period with redundancy payments to which they are entitled, but they will receive the in-lieu payment less any time worked during the notice of termination of employment period.

6.6 Employees who elect to work up to the final day of any 'programme' may do so upon written request, but their in-lieu-of-notice payment will be reduced by the number of weeks worked whilst under notice.

6.7 Employees who are requested by management in writing to remain at work during their notice period will not lose any in-lieu-of-notice entitlement for the period of request.

6.8 The final date of any programme will be stated at the onset of any such programme – the date will normally coincide with the period required by the Department of Employment.

6.9 Employees who are declared redundant and have not either left, been substituted or been given alternative employment by the end of the programme will have their employment terminated on the last date of the programme.

6.10 Should insufficient volunteers be forthcoming, then the person initially selected for redundancy will be the person whose employment will be terminated.

7.0 *Re-engagement*

7.1 All employees covered by the Joint Trade Union Council if made compulsorily redundant will be placed on a recall register. There will be an overall register maintained by the company and each union involved will have a copy of the section of the register that relates to that union.

7.2 Where a vacancy arises, the following will apply:

7.2.1 The opportunity will be given of internal appointment first of all.

7.2.2 Where a vacancy still exists following 7.2.1 above, the recall register for the group involved will be jointly scrutinized and management will decide if there is a suitable recruit.

7.2.3 If, following evaluation under 7.2.2 above, there is still no apparent recruit, the recall register for other trade groups party to this agreement may be considered in order to find a recruit.

7.2.4 If the above steps are unsuccessful, management may recruit from external sources.

7.3 Ex-employees on the recall register will be considered for re-engagement but this is not a guarantee, there is no automatic recall. Individuals on the register will be considered by a joint group, but all decisions will be made by management.

7.4 Management reserves the right, where necessary, and following consultation, to condense the above procedure where time is an important constraint on the recruitment procedure.

7.5 Individuals made compulsorily redundant will have priority consideration for re-engagement for a period of one year from the date of exit. Where individuals are re-engaged in this manner, they will receive continuous service entitlement, except for redundancy entitlement, which will commence from the date of re-engagement.

7.6 Continuous service only applies to individuals re-engaged within one year of being made compulsorily redundant.

8.0 *Items for employees declared redundant*

8.1 The management will give opportunity to employees to find alternative work by:

- Allowing reasonable time off to attend interviews.
- Wherever possible giving early release for those who have jobs outside the company.
- Involving the Department of Employment and Manpower Services Commission.
- Allowing transfers to take place wherever practical with employees who wish to volunteer in other areas (see 3.4 and 4.3).

8.2 *Life assurance cover*
Employees may have their Pension Plan life assurance cover extended for a period of one year, provided:

- They do not take refund of pension contributions from the date of redundancy, and
- They are not in receipt of a Goodyear pension at any time during the one-year period.

8.3 *Pension benefits on redundancy*
Redundancy employees will be entitled to receive one of the following:

8.3.1 A deferred pension payable at age 65 (60 for females) covering the scale entitlement to the date of redundancy.

8.3.2 A return of member contributions if the member has not completed five years of pensionable service. If the member has completed five or more years' pensionable service a refund of contributions paid to 6 April 1975.

8.3.3 Benefits held in the plan may, where negotiable, be transferred to a future employer's scheme.

Appendix: Redundancy terms

A. *Elements of payment*
Redundancy terms for employees are made up of the following payments:

A.1 Statutory redundancy.

A.2 Payment in lieu of notice (see B.1 below and clause 6 of main agreement).

A.3 The company supplementary payment where appropriate.

NB. Outstanding holiday pay is part of an individual's entitlement on leaving the company and this is not considered part of the redundancy terms.

B. *General notes*

B.1 Where management has agreed to accept volunteers for redundancy, payment in lieu of notice will be made in full, provided the employee terminates on the date nominated by management.

Where such a date falls within the 'period of notice' required from the company by the Secretary of State, agreement in principle will be obtained from the appropriate trade union group.

B.2 The tax status of payments made under the redundancy terms are a matter for individuals. In principle, statutory redundancy payments are tax-free but all other payments are subject to individual ruling by the Inland Revenue, but may be tax-free as well.

C. *The company supplementary payment*

C.1 The company agrees to make supplementary payment over and above payments made under the Redundancy Payments Act for those taking redundancy.

C.2 The supplementary payment will be calculated on contractual earnings based on the same period as that used in the calculation of the statutory redundancy element.

D. *The redundancy benefits plan*

D.1 Payment for those employees made redundant will be on the following basis:

D.1.1 *Service element*

One and a half weeks per year of continuous company service.

D.1.2 *Age element*

Age 18–30	4 weeks
31–40	8 weeks
41–50	16 weeks
51–59 women 51–64 men	20 weeks

D.1.3 *Lieu of notice*

In accordance with legislation.

D.2 *Notes:*

- Entitlement under D.1–3 above will be added together to complete the total 'package'.
- The combination of D.1–2 above minus the statutory redundancy payment gives the company supplementary payment.
- Redundancy payment as determined in D.1–2 above will be reduced by one twelfth for each full month past the 64th birthday for men and the 59th birthday for women.
- Weeks of redundancy pay plus weeks of pay in lieu of notice will not exceed weeks of pay to normal retirement date.

D.3 *Additional early retirement benefits*

D.3.1 These benefits are available for those employees who volunteer for redundancy and are eligible to retire early under their respective pension plan rules.

D.3.2 The benefits are:

- Life assurance cover will continue for five years or until normal retirement date if earlier.
- There is no actuarial reduction of pension for early retirement within five years of normal retirement date.
- Where applicable, pensionable service will be credited up to normal retirement date, subject to a maximum of five years.

D.3.3 Under the early retirement plan the total of Goodyear pension, before any cash communication, redundancy pay and pay in lieu of notice must not exceed 80 per cent of pay from leaving date to normal retirement date.

E. *Conditions governing employees who volunteer for redundancy*

E.1 Management agrees to consider applications from employees who wish to volunteer for redundancy in those 'departments' and/or 'defined categories of employees' where it has been announced that personnel reductions are to be achieved. In certain circumstances applications from other 'departments' will also be considered.

E.2 It is agreed that, in considering the applications from those employees who volunteer for redundancy, the following facts will be taken into account:

E.2.1 The manpower requirements of specific functions.

E.2.2 The skill and qualifications required to perform the particular functions, including the possibility of providing skills through training or retraining.

E.2.3 The ability of individual employees within a particular 'department'.

E.3 In exceptional circumstances the management will consider an application from an employee in a 'department' not affected by the reduction but this will only be accepted if the volunteer's position can be effectively filled without increasing the overall manning levels.

It is agreed that, after due consideration of the trade union's view, management will be the sole judge of whether effective transfers will be made.

E.4 The management has the right, after due consideration of the trade union's view, to refuse any applications from employees who volunteer for redundancy.

E.5 When the personnel reductions have been achieved, the management will inform the trade unions and then employees that the redundancy exercise has been completed in the 'department' and no more volunteers are required.

[*Reproduced by courtesy of Goodyear Tyre & Rubber Co. (Great Britain) Ltd, Charles Corfield, Personnel Director*]

Appendix 2

The CV: before and after

Tombstone style

The data are based on a real CV but have been made confidential.

Name	Raymond J. James
Date of birth	13 September 1941
Place of birth	Carlton, Yorkshire
Status	Married; one child aged twelve years
Address	7 Erin Road, Ardingly, West Sussex WS2 3ER
Telephone	Haywards Heath (0444) 000000
Education	
1952–56	Kings School, Pontefract Certificate passes in Maths, English, History and French
1956–57	Royal Navy Communications School Passes in Radio Theory, Wireless Telegraphy and Navigation
Career	Details below
Hobbies/interests	Reading, badminton, horse riding

Work experience

1956–73 *Royal Navy*. Joining as a trainee in communications, leaving as a Radio Supervisor. In this position I was responsible for ships' communication teams.

1973–75 *European Satellite Control Centre, Darmstadt, West Germany*. Employed on contract as a Communications Officer operating worldwide tracking station communications.

1975–78 *Lusaka International Airport, Zambia*. Employed on contract by the Ministry of Overseas Aid as Communications Officer teaching Zambian nationals aeronautical communication and operating civil aviation systems.

1979–84 *Racal Milgo, Doncaster.* Employed originally as a clerk. From this post I progressed through the following positions: Office Manager, Administration Manager and finally Commercial Manager. Prior to leaving I had twenty-one staff and was responsible for the following in five offices located throughout the UK: order processing, invoicing, sales administration, service administration, all contracts, buildings and building services, stock control, installation and maintenance co-ordination. I eventually left owing to low salary of £8,500 p.a.

1985–88 *Wyvern Access Control, Warminster.* Employed originally as Service Manager, responsible for the installation and servicing of industrial security systems throughout Europe. I was promoted to Customer Services Manager, responsible for the preceding, together with internal sales administration and eventually for the sales force as well. I then worked as Sales Manager with design, selling and project control. Salary on leaving Wyvern was £11,500 p.a.

March 1988–December 19xx *Jackson Access Control Systems, Burgess Hill, West Sussex.* Employed as Sales and Marketing Manager. This was a start-up situation, where Jackson had just bought an American manufacturer of access control equipment. I set up the UK marketing, advertising and sales team. This included training the staff in the products and selling techniques. I also had responsibility for engineering and development of products. I left Jackson owing to lack of confidence in the company. Salary was £23,000 p.a. plus bonus.

Achievement style

Raymond J. James
7 Erin Road
Ardingly
West Sussex W82 3ER
Tel. Haywards Heath (0444) 000000

Career and achievements to date

Technical Sales and Marketing Manager, Jackson Access Control Systems, Burgess Hill — March 1988

Responsibilities and achievements

- Set up, trained and managed UK technical sales teams and support staff within start-up budget of £640,000.
- Devised, developed and implemented marketing policies, including PR advertising literature and exhibition work.
- Opened up European markets.
- Devised software support systems.

Sales Manager Wyvern Access Control, Warminster — 1985–88

Responsibilities and achievements

- Through my sales team effected 21 per cent increase in sales within a two-year period.
- Restructured customer services and gained £57,000 new service contracts within six months of take-over.
- Introduced computer control and reporting systems for management information.
- Reduced customer repayments from 100 days to 47 days.
- Designed and managed project control procedures on installations up to £550,000.

Commercial Manager, Racal Milgo, Doncaster — 1979–84

Responsibilities and achievements

- Set up area offices in Birmingham, Manchester and Edinburgh (location search, negotiation, installation and staffing).
- Effected a turnover of £0.5 million within four years.

- Established invoicing and credit control procedures.
- Managed twenty-one staff.

Earlier experience

Lusaka International Airport Authority 1975–78
Communications Officer

European Satellite Control Centre 1973–75
Communications Officer

Royal Navy 1955–73
Radio Supervisor

Education

Royal Navy Communications School
Radio Theory, Wireless, Telegraphy, Navigation.

Kings School, Pontefract
Certificate passes in Maths, English, History and French.

Interests

Riding, badminton at club level, reading, especially historical novels.

Personal details

Date of birth: 13 September 1941
Status: married.
Children: one daughter.
Nationality: British.
Health: excellent.
Height: 6 ft 1½ in.
Weight: 13 st 8 lb.

Appendix 3
Codes of practice

Because of the nature and possible outcomes that arise from outplacement and careers work, it is essential that the highest standards should be maintained. Individuals who are released are often traumatized and in no state to make decisions about their future. When they have overcome their initial shock the career decisions they are called upon to make are perhaps the most significant in their working lives. Employers need to know that their employees are in the hands of professionals who will deal competently with the myriad problems that occur internally and externally when people are forcibly released.

The first attempt at a code of practice was proposed in 1976 by a group called PECCA (Professional and Executive Career Counsellors' Association), only to re-emerge from CMCA (CEPEC Managers Counselling Association), which has about 250 members. This code was endorsed by some of the major concerns in corporate outplacement, the member companies being CEPEC, Coutts, Focus, Hay and Sanders & Sidney. The CODE (Corporate Outplacement Declaration of Ethics) is reproduced below. It is obviously written from the viewpoint of corporate providers of outplacement, as section 3 would exclude any consultancy operating on the retail side of the business, where it is the individual counselled who pays for the service.

Corporate Outplacement Declaration of Ethics

1. The counselling provided will be of a high degree of competence to enable individuals to overcome the stress inherent in the situation and to attain the next stage in their careers but not to act as an employment agency.
2. The outplacement services, programme, support and duration to be provided to individuals shall be agreed in

advance with the sponsoring organization and the individuals.
3. Fees are payable by the sponsoring organization and not by the individual.
4. All information received from clients and individuals shall be treated in the strictest confidence and will not be disclosed to any third party without prior authorization or except as required by law.
5. The education, experience and training of all professional staff and consultants retained by the company will be disclosed.
6. An outplacement organization will receive fees only from its corporate clients and from no other source.
7. No individuals will be knowingly accepted into an outplacement programme if they need medical/psychological therapy beyond the competence of the outplacement consultancy unless parallel medical/psychiatric support is provided.

There is a debate in the industry as to which is more ethical – corporate or retail. Corporate protagonists claim that it is somehow not acceptable to take fees from individuals and point out that in retail there is no redress should the individual receive poor service. Retail would claim that, if the service is valid and beneficial, individuals with career difficulties ought to be able to purchase it particularly and especially when their employer will not or cannot provide this proven benefit. As far as redress is concerned, the reputation of the retail consultancy is at stake. Although the main object of a code of practice is to protect the interest of the individual, there is a certain commercial cachet in the exclusivity that a code would bring.

The retail sector has its own code, published under the auspices of the International Association of Outplacement Professionals (IAOP). Interexec, the largest of the retail outplacement providers in the UK, have done much to nurture the code, adherents of which are growing in number in the UK and abroad. The code arose from concern that several states of the USA had banned outplacement because of the activities of unscrupulous operators. Both the code promoted by CEPEC and the IAOP code of practice can trace their roots back to an attempt by the industry to regulate its own activities.

In 1991 the Institute of Personnel Management published its own Code of Conduct for Career and Outplacement Consultants (below). As with the other codes the IPM document seeks to safeguard the interests of users. It addresses the needs of both the corporate sector (which it calls sponsored services) and the retail sector (which it calls private services).

At the time of writing it has yet to be seen how effective any of these codes will be in ensuring a high-calibre service to those made redundant. Much will depend on how services are policed and how far clients, both corporate and individual, use the codes in selecting the consultants with whom they work. The IPM code is the only one which addresses the problem of policing in a comprehensive manner.

Background

The IPM recognizes that a significant number of its members are engaged in the provision of consultancy services. The aim of this code is to develop professional standards for those engaged in career and outplacement consultancy to promote and maintain high levels of professional conduct.

This code is not intended to be a substitute for more detailed good practice policies adopted by individual organizations, provided they at least meet the requirements set out here.

It is accepted that, as members of the Institute, career and outplacement consultants should also adhere to and be aware of the standards detailed in the IPM's Code of Professional Conduct, Recruitment Code, Code of Occupational Testing, Redundancy Code and Equal Opportunities Code. They should also be aware of the guidelines in the IPM Statement on Age and Employment.

Introduction to this code

The IPM recognizes that career and outplacement consultancy services can be divided into:

- *Sponsored services* – where the 'client' is an organization paying for services provided to an individual or group of individuals, and
- *Private services* – where services are provided to clients as individuals paying for the services they personally receive.

This code is intended to address both types of activities and therefore contains two sections. Section 1 refers specifically to sponsored career and outplacement consultancy services and section 2 to private career and outplacement activity.

This code is not intended to apply to people providing careers advice for which no payment is received, for example members of the careers advisory service or school careers officers.

Explanation of terms used in this code

Consultants
Individuals engaged in providing either career or outplacement services. (The role of the consultant is essentially specified in the section on the professional relationship between consultants and clients.)

Consultancy
Organizations providing either career or outplacement services. (The role of the consultancy is essentially specified in the section on the business relationship between consultants and clients.)

Consultancies must ensure their consultants adhere to the provisions of this code.

Career and outplacement consultants
People who provide counselling and services to enable

individuals to develop a greater awareness of their capacities, skills and limitations, to identify and pursue the career opportunities open to them and to manage the transition through a career change or into re-employment following loss of job. Career consultants may not be specifically concerned with outplacement.

Section 1. Sponsored career and outplacement services

A. *Business relationship between consultant, client buying services and individual receiving services*

Advertising

- All advertisements will comply with the Code of Advertising Practice.
- The content of all advertisements and public relations material will be unambiguous, accurate and capable of being verified.
- All oral representations to prospective clients and individuals will be unambiguous and accurate.
- All claims regarding past performance of a career or outplacement consultancy will be capable of verification.

Nature of the contract

- The contractual relationship and services to be made available, including their duration, will be agreed and confirmed in writing to the client.
- A copy of the contract will be supplied to the individual receiving services.
- The contract will run either for a specified length of time or until the individual is re-employed; in the latter case, the assignment may be concluded if the consultants can demonstrate they can no longer be of assistance to the individual. Such a decision must only be taken in consultation with and with the agreement of the individual and the client.

- Consultants should ensure clients and individuals are aware at the commencement of the contract that consultants cannot guarantee successful placement into new employment.
- Any other guarantees must be set out in advance in a written contract to the client copied to the individual.
- The consultants who will provide the services will be identified in the contract and any subsequent changes will take place only in consultation with the individual and the client.

Payment

- Fees and terms of payment will be disclosed to the client in writing in advance. Furthermore, details of what is included in the fees must be given.
- Consultants will allow individuals a fourteen day 'cooling-off period', during which the consultancy would, on the client's request to terminate services, charge only for work actually done, in lieu of any fixed, larger or composite fees which might have been anticipated. Clients and individuals must be given a clear indication in advance of the charges involved should they decide to terminate the contract within this period of fourteen days.
- A schedule of payments with clear indications of when monies will fall due will be agreed with clients in writing at commencement of the contract.
- Consultants will not make additional charges to clients above those fees originally agreed at commencement of the contract nor make charges to any other party in connection with the individual or assignment, except as originally disclosed or subsequently agreed with the client and confirmed in writing.

General

- Consultancies will not engage in any unlawful restraint of trade or unfair method of competition.
- Consultancies must maintain professional indemnity insurance.

B. *Professional relationship between consultant, client paying for services and individual receiving services*

Qualifications

- Consultants must be able to demonstrate that they possess a minimum level of competence in the provision of outplacement and career consultancy services by possessing one of the following:
  - Corporate membership of the IPM.
  - A qualification in psychology, vocational guidance or counselling recognized by a professional body such as the British Psychological Society.
  - A range of knowledge and experience equivalent to that specified in the guidelines for IPM membership under the management entry scheme for this specialism.
- Psychometric testing and feedback must only be conducted by holders of the British Psychological Society Statement or Certificate of Competence in Psychological Testing.[1]
- Consultants must be willing to give details of their qualifications and experience on request from the client or individual.

Acceptance of individuals for counselling

- Consultants will not accept any individuals for counselling without holding an initial meeting of sufficient duration with the individual or the client to enable the consultant to achieve a clear understanding of their requirements. It will be made clear to clients that this meeting is without commitment by either party. Such a meeting must be free of charge.
- No individual will be knowingly accepted into a counselling programme if it is evident they need medical/ psychological therapy beyond the competence of the

[1] Effective from July 1991.

consultant or the resources available. Such therapy may be provided by other agencies at the same time.

- Consultants will not accept any individual where the services they can make available are unlikely to contribute substantially to the achievement of the individual's objectives.
- Any known or potential conflict of interest will be divulged before an assignment is accepted.
- Consultants will always act in the best interests of the individual and this will be communicated to clients.

Provision of services

- If an individual is submitted for a vacancy which is being handled by an associated recruitment service of the career or outplacement consultancy, then the nature of the association must be disclosed to both the individual and the client of the associated recruitment service.
- Consultants will take all reasonable steps to ensure that adequate information is obtained regarding the individual's background and abilities, to provide a firm foundation for any personal career advice given. This should include in-depth interviewing, bio-data and references, and may include psychometric testing.
- Consultants must be able to demonstrate effective quality control in their activities and specify quality control methods.
- Information received from clients and individuals shall be treated in the strictest confidence and will not be disclosed to any third party without prior authorization.
- Individuals have the right to expect that appropriate communication will be maintained with them throughout the assignment. For example, contact should take place at least once a month, when individuals must be advised of all activities undertaken on their behalf.
- Consultants will remain independent of clients' and individuals' affairs and the opportunities they seek to

pursue, to ensure that counsel and advice remain objective throughout the assignment. Any actual or potential conflict of interest should be disclosed as soon as it is recognized by the consultant.

General

- Consultants must be fully aware of and comply with the relevant employment legislation affecting the provision of services. Breach of the law will be deemed a breach of this code.

Section 2. Private career and outplacement services

A. *Business relationship between consultant and client receiving services*

Advertising

- All advertisements will comply with the Code of Advertising Practice.
- The content of all advertisements and public relations material will be unambiguous, accurate and capable of being verified.
- All oral representations to prospective clients and individuals will be unambiguous and accurate.
- All claims regarding past performance of a career or outplacement consultancy will be capable of verification.

Nature of the contract

- The contractual relationship and services to be made available, including their duration, will be agreed and confirmed in writing.
- The contract will run either for a specified length of time or until the client is re-employed; in the latter case, the assignment may be concluded if the consultants can demonstrate they can no longer be of assis-

tance to the client. Such a decision must only be taken in consultation with and with the agreement of the client.

- Consultants should ensure clients are aware at commencement of the contract that consultants cannot guarantee successful placement into new employment.
- Any other guarantees must be set out in advance in a written contract.
- The consultants who will provide the services will be identified in the contract and any subsequent changes will take place only in consultation with the client.

Payment

- Fees and terms of payment will be disclosed to the client in writing in advance. Furthermore, details of what is included in the fees must be given.
- Consultants will allow clients a fourteen day 'cooling-off period', during which the consultancy would, on the client's request to terminate services, charge only for work actually done, in lieu of any fixed, larger or composite fees which might have been anticipated. Clients must be given a clear indication in advance of the charges involved should they decide to terminate the contract within this period of fourteen days.
- Consultants must not ask clients to make any payment exceeding the costs expected to accrue during the fourteen-day 'cooling-off period' until, at least, fourteen days into the contract.
- A schedule of payments with clear indications of when monies will fall due will be agreed with clients in writing at commencement of the contract.
- Consultants will not make additional charges to clients above those fees originally agreed at commencement of the contract nor make charges to any other party in connection with the client or assignment, except as originally disclosed or subsequently agreed with the client and confirmed in writing.

General

- Consultancies will not engage in any unlawful restraint of trade or unfair method of competition.
- Consultancies must maintain professional indemnity insurance.

B. *Professional relationship between consultant and client receiving services*

Qualifications

- Consultants must be able to demonstrate that they possess a minimum level of competence in the provision of outplacement and career consultancy services by possessing one of the following:
  - Corporate membership of the IPM.
  - A qualification in psychology, vocational guidance or counselling recognized by a professional body such as the British Psychological Society.
  - A range of knowledge and experience equivalent to that specified in the guidelines for IPM membership under the management entry scheme for this specialism.
- Psychometric testing and feedback must only be conducted by holders of the British Psychological Society Statement or Certificate of Competence in Psychological Testing.[1]
- Consultants must be willing to give details of their qualifications and experience on request from the client or individual.

Acceptance of clients for counselling

- Consultants will not accept a client for counselling without holding an initial meeting of sufficient duration to enable the consultant to achieve a clear understanding of the client's requirements. It will be made clear

[1] Effective from July 1991.

to clients that this meeting is without commitment by either party. Such a meeting must be free of charge.

- No client will be knowingly accepted into a counselling programme if it is evident they need medical/ psychological therapy beyond the competence of the consultant or the resources available. Such therapy may be provided by other agencies at the same time.
- Consultants will not accept a client where the services they can make available are unlikely to contribute substantially to the achievement of the client's objectives.
- Any known or potential conflict of interests will be divulged before an assignment is accepted.

Provision of services

- If a client is submitted for a vacancy which is being handled by an associated recruitment service of the career or outplacement consultancy, then the nature of the association must be disclosed to the client of the outplacement consultancy and the client of the associated recruitment service.
- Consultants will take all reasonable steps to ensure that adequate information is obtained regarding the client's background and abilities, to provide a firm foundation for any personal career advice given. This should include indepth interviewing, bio-data and references, and may include psychometric testing.
- Consultants must be able to demonstrate effective quality control in their activities and specify quality control methods.
- Information received from clients shall be treated in the strictest confidence and will not be disclosed to any third party without prior authorization.
- Clients have the right to expect that appropriate communication will be maintained with them throughout the assignment. For example, contact should take place at least once a month, when clients must be advised of all activities undertaken on their behalf.

- Consultants will remain independent of clients' affairs and the opportunities they seek to pursue, to ensure that counsel and advice remain objective throughout the assignment. Any actual or potential conflict of interest should be disclosed as soon as it is recognized by the consultant.

General

- Consultants must be fully aware of and comply with the relevant employment legislation affecting the provision of services. Breach of the law will be deemed a breach of this code.

Section 3. Action to be taken in the light of possible unprofessional conduct

The Institute has recently reviewed its Code of Professional Conduct and Ethics following an extensive consultation exercise at branch and regional level. The code was approved and adopted by Council on 17 May 1991, but will require the consent of the general membership to a change in the Institute's Articles of Association.

In the meantime, the code as approved will form the basis upon which all members of the Institute will be expected to maintain the highest standards of professionalism in the field of personnel management. Therefore, queries and/or disputes arising from the implementation of the Code of Conduct for Career and Outplacement Consultants will be investigated and decided according to the Professional Conduct Regulations referred to above.

These regulations provide for a disciplinary panel chaired by the immediate past president assisted by between two and four other senior members of the Institute. Specialist advisers may be co-opted. There is also an appeal panel of the President and four honorary officers.

The powers of the disciplinary panel range from dismissing a complaint, through warning a member to expulsion. The panel will also make recommendations to the President regarding publication of the decision.

A complaint against a member can be made by the Institute, another member or a third party. The circumstances of the complaint should be made in writing, under confidential cover, to the Secretary of the Institute at IPM House.

The Code of Conduct can be obtained by sending a s.a.e. to the Marketing Department, IPM House, Camp Road, Wimbledon, London SW19 4UX.

Glossary

Achievement list A list of all the successes and achievements in an individual's career so that information can be quantified for CV and interview purposes.

Achievement word Action verb in the immediate past tense or '-ed' form, e.g. 'manag*ed*', 'creat*ed*', design*ed*', 'implement*ed*'.

Advice centre Alternative form of Job Centre when unemployment in the locality is so high that getting a job is unlikely.

Alligator Outplacement slang: an individual who enjoys all the outplacement facilities a firm offers and is still discontented.

Bail-out (1) Key executive who, although in a secure job, leaves the restructured organization. (2) Government help to a firm or organization.

Behaviour modelling Providing individuals with behaviour or people to copy, e.g. how to behave at interview – or how to appear confident.

Belly-up Term used when a firm goes bust or when an individual gives up looking for a job.

Billfold biopsy US outplacement slang: checking to see whether the individual can afford the service required.

Blanket As in 'sandpaper and blankets'. Blankets are given as a reward for work well done or for effort. (see *sandpaper*.)

Bleeding head/skull An individual on a headhunter's short list who is in employment at the time of presentation.

Body shops Agencies which treat employers like a coconut shy – throw enough balls (people) at the coconut (job) and it will be knocked down (filled).

Boilerplate language Puff in an outplacement proposal. Standard stuff that appears in every tender or proposal.

Break-out area Discussion area for participants on a training programme.

Broken When a person gives up looking for jobs.

Brown-eyed boy list Subjective list of the people a manager would like to make redundant.

Bumping When someone's job is made redundant and they are entitled to return to their previous job, from which they were promoted, and thus bump that person into redundancy.

Buzz group Small sub-group of training participants separated out specifically to solve a problem.

Career statement A twenty-or-so-word sentence that encapsulates what the individual potential employee has to offer.

Chinese wall Organizational barrier; term borrowed from finance where brokerage and underwriting are separated. When an outplacement agency and a recruitment agency are jointly managed it needs an impenetrable barrier between the two.

Coat-tailing Always ending on a positive note when an interviewee is forced into giving negative information.

Corporate outplacement Outplacement services paid for by organizations and not by the individuals themselves. (The latter is known as retail.)

Criteria interviewing A set of predetermined standards based upon the job requirements which are used as the basis of the interview.

CV (*Curriculum vitae*) A written outline of an individual career history.

Deadheading Promoting an able junior person over an established job holder.

Dear John Employers' refusal letter to an applicant.

Decruitment Going through the motions of recruitment for

the sake of image but not actually taking anyone on.

Dehiring Making the conditions and work of an employee so difficult that they resign of their own accord.

Ding letter Employers' refusal letter. Cf 'Dear John', 'PTD'.

Downsizing Reducing manpower by redundancy to a smaller head count.

Dual ladder Where specialists and technical people can have the same status and pay as managers. A method of rewarding technical excellence.

Executive search Recruitment method whereby individuals who are in work but meet another employer's requirement are sought out by the recruiter, or headhunter.

Exit interview Discussion with employer's representative before an individual leaves an organization.

Face validity How much a test or questionnaire looks as if it will measure what it says it is attempting to measure.

Fat contract Where the employer wishes to release lots of people and give them outplacement over a very short period.

Fatigue curve Diagrammatic representation of when an employee is at their best or worse over a given time span.

Fats Letters of offer from an employer; fat because the envelope usually bulges with two copies of the contract of employment, one for the employee and the other for the firm.

FIFO (1) First In, First Out. (2) When giving psychological questionnaires, telling candidates that Fantasy In gets Fantasy Out.

Focus groups Groups of participants who have gone through an outplacement programme who are brought together to see how the programme can be improved.

Front end The beginning of an outplacement programme.

Gardening leave (1) A procrastinating activity sometimes taken up by those made redundant – they would rather garden than look for work. (2) Employees who are told not to come in to work because there is none for them to do, usually whilst 'working' extended notice.

Gatekeepers People in the organization who cannot give someone a job but through whom an applicant has to pass – thus gatekeeper.

Give-back A management demand for reduced pay and benefits because of an adverse trading position or some other difficulty. A way of avoiding job losses.

Golden hallo A lump sum and benefits to induce someone to join a firm.

Golden handcuffs Pay at the ninety-fifth percentile and above, that is, so high that the recipient cannot afford to leave the organization.

Golden handshake A lump sum and benefits to encourage voluntary retirement.

Golden parachute (1) A contractual way of protecting top executives in the event of an unwelcome take-over. (2) Agreement at the beginning of employment on generous separation terms, including outplacement, should the appointment go wrong.

Group programmes Outplacement training for two or more people.

Heavy hitter Outplacement slang for a top-paid executive for a one-to-one programme who brings significant fee income based on a percentage of the final salary.

Hinge A method of connecting a personal achievement to the potential benefit of the employer; particularly used in CVs and during the selection interview.

Hot button Whatever is likely to make an individual attractive to a potential employer, and vice versa.

Hygienes Those things which are a prerequisite to job satisfaction and personal growth, such as adequate pay, canteen, etc.

Interest battery A questionnaire (or series of) which identifies an individual's job preferences.

Job Centre Government agency-run job shop which makes no charge to employers or employees.

Job lead Information that might assist a person to get a job.

Job loading Increasing an individual's work responsibilities but not promoting them to a higher job, status or grade.

Job lunching (1) Part of the networking process. Taking people to lunch who can give you a job or a lead to one. (2) Being taken out to lunch by a prospective employer.

Job posting Vacancy lists of positions available within the firm, intended primarily to encourage promotion from within.

Job shop An on-site facility set up by an outplacement consultancy to find local jobs for employees who are being released and provide support and training for them in their job search.

Lateral move A sideways move for an executive. Usually an early sign of failure or poor performance.

Launch In outplacement terms, the opening of a job shop for the employees and any associated PR activity.

Letting go Part of the job loss process where the employee no longer looks back at the job he or she held but forward to the job(s) he or she can get.

LIFO Last In, First Out. The accepted redundancy formula in the absence of any other policy or precedent for release.

Loyalty bonus/payments A cash sum given at the end of the notice period given specifically to encourage redundant employees not to leave until the end of the period.

MBTI Myers Briggs Type Indicator, a personality questionnaire much favoured by outplacement consultancies.

Member A term adopted by Pauline Hyde to describe a person going through outplacement. It helps to distinguish the person from the client who pays the member's fees.

Mind mapping A creativity technique developed by Tony

Buzan to help an individual use his or her creative skills. Used in outplacement to discover themes and options for the individual.

Missionary selling Presenting outplacement services to organizations who have never heard of it before.

Monkey A problem. Whoever has the problem has the monkey. Most used in outplacement during negotiations for the starting rate.

Networking The process of contacting friends, colleagues and others with the sole purpose of creating or hearing of a job opportunity.

NLP Neuro-linguistic programming, an interpersonal skills system developed by Richard Bander and John Grinder.

Non-directive A form of counselling where the individual is helped to take full responsibility for a difficulty and its resolution.

Offer evaluation Comparing the advantages of one job offer with those of another with a view to making a choice.

Open question The most common type of question asked by interviewers. Usually begins with 'What', 'How', 'Why' or 'Tell me'.

Pay for knowledge Additional job information given to an employee over and above the job requirements which facilitates productivity.

Phatic language Soft words to help employee accept bad news.

Pick-up An interview with an outplacement counsellor held immediately after the individual has been told of his or her redundancy.

Pole position Best position. Best position for interview is to have the penultimate interview of the day.

Primacy effect An interviewer's first impression of a candidate. Research suggests that it is the most powerful impression in terms of what the interviewer remembers.

Principal questions These are the three questions suggested by Robert Half as the major questions at interviews: 'Can this person do the job?' 'Will this person do the job?' 'Will this person fit in?'

Promo-speak A way of talking which promotes the speaker rather than the listener or the topic of conversation. A necessary skill in outplacement.

Psych. pay A benefit which is perceived by the individual as deriving from the job over and above remuneration, such as status, satisfaction, self-actualization, etc.

Psychometrics Tests and questionnaires which furnish psychological data about the individuals who complete them.

PTD Polite turn-downs: employers' refusal letters.

Quit rate $\frac{\text{Voluntary leavers over a year}}{\bar{x}\text{ employees in a year}} \times \frac{100}{1}$

Rainbow job Fantasy job. Sometimes outplaced employees are encouraged to go for something they have only dreamt about.

Recency effect The last impression an applicant leaves with an interviewer. The second most significant (after the primary effect).

Red circle A job which for historical reasons enjoys a higher rate of pay than it should.

Red thumb A job which has a higher rate of pay than it should and is being held at that rate until other jobs on the same grade catch up through normal pay reviews.

Redundantee A person who held a job which has become redundant and is therefore no longer employed.

Release Euphemism for 'fire', 'make redundant' or 'sack'.

Releasing manager The manager who carries out the termination interview of the person whose job is redundant.

Repertory grid A technique devised by G. A. Kelly for exploring an individual's constructs or the way he or she views and understands the world. A powerful outplacement counselling technique.

Resource centre A name developed by TDA for an on-site job shop facility held to assist employees being released.

Retail outplacement Outplacement services which are paid for by the individual recipient.

Retail therapy Going on a spending spree with the separation payment to help ease the hurt of job loss.

Revolving door Taking employees on, using them and releasing them quickly.

Rifle shot A letter specifically aimed 'cold' at a chosen target firm.

Rogerian A form of non-directive counselling after the style of Carl Rogers.

RPA Redundancy Payments Act.

Rust-out Opposite of burn-out; where an employee suffers anxiety or stress through doing an undemanding and boring job.

Sandpaper Opposite of 'blanket'. To encourage the out-placed person to work harder at job search first by firm talking to and then by being demanding.

Separation payment Payment made in excess of the statutory minimum.

Severance pay The term has a variety of meanings. Most popular is total contractual entitlements on leaving.

Shake-out Euphemism for releasing non-performing or non-contributing employees.

Shopper An outplacement candidate in either corporate or retail who visits several consultancies before deciding which to use.

Skills inventory A list of an individual's skills and abilities.

SME Subject-matter expert – much loved by outplacement consultancies because for the most part easy to place elsewhere.

Spiral down Rubbish the employer who made one's job redundant during the course of an interview.

Squeaky wheel An outplacement candidate who discovers that the more you complain the better service you get. See 'alligator'.

Strategic counselling A form of counselling where the counsellor knows the direction in which the client should be moving and actively helps him/her in that direction without making it obvious.

Stroking A TA term; giving an individual a reward of some kind which can be either conditional or unconditional.

SWOT Strengths, Weaknesses, Opportunities and Threats.

TA Transactional analysis. A way of understanding self and the interaction of others. Developed by Eric Berne.

Targeting Identification of potential jobs or job sectors by a job searcher.

Tele-marketing (1) Canvassing for jobs over the phone by a job searcher. (2) Canvassing for clients over the phone by consultancies.

Terminal job (1) Position from which there is no promotion. (2) First job for new graduate expected to leave or move on in a set period.

Thematic Type of CV where abilities, skills and experience are drawn together rather than set out chronologically.

Thick project The release of a lot of people all at the same time, requiring a lot of outplacement counsellors on-site.

Thin Polite turn-down (PTD), Dear John; polite letter of refusal by an employer.

Thin project An outplacement contract where employees are released gradually rather than quickly; the opposite of a thick contract.

Tombstone A CV which gives every detail in strict chronological sequence.

Transition The process by which the individual passes from job loss to settling into new career.

Transplacement Help to employees to find a job elsewhere; can also mean career and job search assistance for the spouse.

Trial by sherry A group meeting of aspiring applicants when they meet the department. Most common in the Health Service and academic appointments.

Triplicate of choice Where, in response to an open question at interview, the interviewee gives three possible topics and invites the interviewer to respond to one of them, thus ensuring that interview time is best utilized.

Use or lose Outplaced employees are encouraged to improve both their physical and mental health on the basis that they will atrophy with minimum use during unemployment.

USP Unique Selling Point – what the candidate has or can offer which makes him or her ideally suited to the position on offer.

Bibliography

M. B. Arthur *et al.*, *Handbook of Career Theory*, Cambridge University Press, 1989

R. B. Baird, *The Executive Experience*, ninth edition, Executive Grapevine, 1990–91

E. Berne, *What Do You Say After You Say Hello?* Deutsch, 1974

M. Broussine and Y. Guerrier, *Surviving as a Middle Manager*, Croom Helm, 1983

A. F. Buono and J. L. Bowditch, *The Human Side of Mergers and Acquisitions*, Jossey-Bass, 1989

T. Buzan, *Make the Most of Your Mind*, Pan, 1977

R. B. Cattell *et al.*, *Handbook for the Sixteen Personality Factor Questionnaire*, NFER, 1970

R. R. Clarkhuff, *The Art of Problem-solving*, Human Resource Development Press, 1974

R. R. Clarkhuff, *How to Help Yourself*, Human Resource Development Press, 1974

S. Fineman, *White Collar Unemployment*, Wiley, 1983

S. Fineman, *Unemployment*, Tavistock, 1987

F. Fransella and D. Bannister, *A Manual for Repertory Grid Technique*, Academic, 1977

E. Goffman, *Stigma*, Prentice-Hall, 1963

A. Goulder, 'The unemployed self', in R. Fraser (ed.), *Work: Twenty Personal Accounts*, Penguin, 1969

C. Grunfeld, *The Law of Redundancy*, Sweet and Maxwell, 1980

R. Half, *The Robert Half Way to Get Hired in Today's Job Market*, Rawson Wade, 1981

O. M. Hall, 'Attitudes of unemployed engineers', *Personnel Journal*, 12 (1933), 222–8

J. Hallett, *Planned Job Search*, Granary, 1988

C. Hardy, *Managing Organisational Closure*, Gower, 1985

J. Hartley and C. L. Cooper, 'Redundancy: a psychological problem?' *Personnel Review*, 5, 44–8

J. Hartley *et al.*, *Job Insecurity*, Sage, 1991

J. Hayes and P. Nutman, *Understanding the Unemployed*, Tavistock, 1981

B. Hopson and J. Adams, 'Towards an understanding of transition', in J. Adams, J. Hayes and B. Hopson (eds), *Transition: understanding and managing personal change*, Martin Robertson, 1976

B. Hopson and M. Scally, *Build your own Rainbow*, Lifeskills Associates, 1984

J. W. Hunt and R. R. Collins, *Managers in Mid-career Crisis*, Wellington Lane, 1983

M. M. Hyman, 'The effects of unemployment: a neglected problem in modern social research', in Merton *et al.*, *Qualitative and Quantitative Social Research*, Free Press

B. Jaffe, *Altered Ambitions*, Fine, 1991

M. Jahoda, 'The impact of unemployment in the 1930's and in the 1970's', *Bulletin of the British Psychological Society*, 32 (1979), 309–14

M. Jahoda, *Employment and Unemployment*, Cambridge University Press, 1982

C. Jenkins and B. Sharman, *The Collapse of Work*, Eyre Methuen

H. R. Kahn, *Repercussions of Redundancy*, Allen & Unwin, 1964

P. KELVIN and J. E. JARRETT, *Unemployment*, Cambridge University Press, 1985

S. E. KRUG, *Interpreting 16PF Profile Patterns*, Institute of Personality Testing, Illinois, 1981

E. KÜBLER-ROSS, *On Death and Dying*, Tavistock, 1969

K. LEGGE, 'Personnel management in recession and recovery: a comparative analysis', *Personnel Review*, 47 (1988), 1–72

H. LEVIE *et al.*, *Fighting Closures*, Spokesman, 1984

H. LEVINSON *et al.*, *Men, Management and Mental Health*, Harvard University Press, 1962

M. R. LOUIS, 'Career transitions: varieties and commonalities', *Academy of Management Review*, 5 (1980), 329–40

J. MACINNES, *Thatcherism at Work*, Open University Press, 1987

J. MARTIN and C. ROBERTS, *Women and Unemployment: a Lifetime Perspective*, HMSO, 1984

M. MEGRANAHAN, *Counselling: a Practical Guide for Employers*, Institute of Personnel Management, 1989

R. T. MOWDAY *et al.*, *Employee–Organisation Linkages*, Academic, 1982

R. MURRAY-THOMAS, *Counselling and Life Span Development*, Sage, 1990

R. NELSON JONES, *Practical Counselling Skills*, Cassell, 1983

R. NELSON-BOLLES, *The 1989 What Color is your Parachute?*, Ten Speed Press, 1989

N. NICHOLSON *et al.*, *The Dynamics of White Collar Unionism*, Academic, 1981

N. NICHOLSON and M. WEST, *Managerial Job Change: Men and Women in Transition*, Cambridge University Press, 1988

G. E. O'BRIEN, *Psychology of Work and Unemployment*, Wiley, 1986

C. M. PARKES, *Bereavement*, Tavistock, 1972

P. Pritchett, *After the Merger: Managing the Shockwaves*, Dow Jones–Irwin, 1985

A. Reed, *Returning to Work: a Practical Guide for Women*, Kogan Page, 1989

A. Rodger, *Seven Point Plan*, National Foundation for Educational Research, 1974

C. R. Rogers, 'The characteristics of a helping relationship', *Personnel and Guidance Journal*, 37, 6–16, 1958

C. R. Rogers, *Client-centered Therapy*, Houghton Mifflin, 1951

E. H. Schein, *Organisational Psychology*, Prentice-Hall, 1965

N. Schlossberg and A. Liebowitz, 'Organisational support systems as buffers to job loss', *Journal of Vocational Behaviour*, 17 (1980), 401–26

M. E. P. Seligman, *Helplessness*, Freeman, 1975

H. Shephard and A. Belitsky, *The Job Hunt*, Johns Hopkins University Press, 1966

B. Spencer, 'Shop steward resistance in the recession', *Employee Relations*, 7 (1985), 22–8

V. Stoikow and R. L. Raimon, 'Determinants of differences in the quit rate among industries', *American Economic Review*, (1968), 1283–98

R. I. Sutton, 'Managing organisational death', *Human Resource Management*, 22 (1983), 391–412

P. Swinburne, 'The psychological impact of unemployment on managers and professional staff', *Journal of Occupational Psychology*, 54 (1981), 47–64

P. R. Timm and D. A. Peterson, *People at Work*, West Publishing Company, 1982

R. M. Tomasko, *Downsizing: Reshaping the Corporation for the Future*, AMACON, 1990

M. Walters, *What About the Workers?: making employee surveys work*, Institute of Personnel Management, 1990

P. B. WARR, 'Job loss, unemployment and well-being', in Allen and Uliert Role, *Transitions Review*, 1984

P. B. WARR, *Work, Unemployment and Mental Health*, Oxford University Press, 1987

B. WISHARD, 'Merger – the human dimension', *Magazine of Bank Administration*, 61, 6 (1985), 76–9

K. S. WOLFER and R. G. WONG, *The Outplacement Solution*, Wilty, 1988

P. T. P. WONG and B. WEINER, 'When people ask "why" questions and the heuristics of attributional search', *Journal of Personality and Social Psychology*, 40, 650–63

M. WOODCOCK and D. FRANCIS, *The Unblocked Manager*, Wildwood House, 1982

C. WOOLFSON and J. FOSTER, *Track Record: the Story of the Caterpillar Occupation*, Verso, 1988

Index